JOHN HENRY NEWMAN

The Uses of Knowledge

Crofts Classics

GENERAL EDITOR

Samuel H. Beer, *Harvard University*

JOHN HENRY NEWMAN

The Uses
of Knowledge

SELECTIONS FROM
THE IDEA OF A UNIVERSITY

EDITED BY
Leo L. Ward

WILEY-BLACKWELL
www.wiley.com/wiley-blackwell

This edition first published 1948
© 1948 Harlan Davidson, Inc.

Harlan Davidson, Inc. was acquired by John Wiley & Sons in May 2012.

Registered Office
John Wiley & Sons Ltd, The Atrium, Southern Gate, Chichester, West Sussex,
PO19 8SQ, UK

Editorial Offices
350 Main Street, Malden, MA 02148-5020, USA
9600 Garsington Road, Oxford, OX4 2DQ, UK
The Atrium, Southern Gate, Chichester, West Sussex, PO19 8SQ, UK

For details of our global editorial offices, for customer services, and for
information about how to apply for permission to reuse the copyright material in
this book please see our website at www.wiley.com/wiley-blackwell.

The right of Leo L. Ward to be identified as the author of the editorial material in
this work has been asserted in accordance with the UK Copyright, Designs and
Patents Act 1988.

Library of Congress Cataloging-in-Publication Data

48-8929
ISBN 0-88295-063-0 (pbk.)
ISBN 978-0-88295-063-1 (pbk.)

contents

Principal Dates in Newman's Life

1801   Birth, London, February 21.

1816   Entered Trinity College, Oxford.

1821   Made Fellow of Oriel College, Oxford.

1824   Ordained in the ministry of the Anglican Church.

1828   Made Vicar of St. Mary's, the University Church, where his sermons soon attracted a large following. His sermons showed the increasing tendency toward traditional doctrine and practice.

1841   Published Tract 90. This was perhaps the high point of what has come to be known as the Oxford Movement, an attempt on the part of Newman and a group of Oxford friends to bring the Church of England back to more traditional doctrines and practices. The Tract was widely read and created new tensions and dissensions in the Anglican Church. Somewhat later Newman gave up his position in Oxford and retired to Littlemore, where he remained, with a small group of friends, in virtual retreat.

1845   Professed faith in the Roman Catholic Church, and, a year later, was ordained in Rome.

1852   After returning to England and establishing a religious house in Birmingham, delivered in Dublin a series of nine lectures in connection with plans for a new Catholic University. These lectures later became, in book form, the first main section of *The Idea of a University*.

1854   Appointed Rector of the Catholic University in Dublin, and delivered the ten lectures which became the second main section of *The Idea of a University*.

1858   Retired from the Rectorship, after meeting delays and difficulties, and misunderstandings on the part of authorities in Ireland.

1864   Wrote his autobiography, *Apologia Pro Vita Sua*.

1879   Made Cardinal by Pope Leo XIII.

1890   Died, August 11, at religious oratory near Birmingham.

introduction

Education seems to have some special importance for Americans. From the earliest days the little log school was looked upon as an indispensable institution in every pioneer community. Since then our educational establishments have grown amazingly in every region of the country, and yet they always seem to remain inadequate to meet the demand. Clearly, knowledge must have some special importance or value for the American mind.

But what is its value? Why do we seek knowledge? What is its utility? We do not seem to have reached any general agreement about the answer to the question. This book presents an answer by John Henry Newman, first made in a series of lectures over a hundred years ago, and later published in a book that has since become a literary and educational classic. The Idea of a University was composed of two main sections, the first of which was entitled "University Teaching," and the second, "University Subjects." In the first section of the book Newman developed the essential outline of his views on university education. Of the nine lectures which made up this first section of the book, four are reprinted here, under a new title, The Uses of Knowledge. From the second section of the book three passages have been added here, in Appendices, to suggest certain amplifications of his thought made by Newman in some of his later lectures.

Because the book from which these four lectures are taken is integrated very closely, as a whole unit of thought, no complete view of Newman's meaning can be grasped from any of the parts. Each of his main ideas, to be fully and justly comprehended, must be seen in the context of the whole book. For this reason the broad scheme of Newman's thought has been presented in a "General Argument." The student is urged to give particular attention to this digest, in order to provide himself with a framework of reference for the study of the four lectures included in the present book. With the help of this General Argument, it is hoped that the student will be able to see these four lectures in their true relationship to the whole of Newman's thought.

Some readers may wish to go back to The Idea of a University in order to see Newman's argument in its complete elaboration. The four lectures which are reproduced here will abundantly reveal his special ability to elaborate and qualify his ideas with a rich texture of precise detail. In this lies some of the peculiar strength of Newman's thought, and one of the special excellences of his style. The reader who becomes aware of this distinction of thought and expression will be led back to the whole book, fully assured of the reward to be found in a complete statement of a great idea.

Why are we seeking knowledge? What is its value? Its utility? If we as students are really concerned, we shall find in Newman's book a very suggestive answer to these questions.

GENERAL ARGUMENT IN THE IDEA
OF A UNIVERSITY

*Brief excerpts stating the essential notions contained in
the Preface and the first nine Discourses*

PREFACE

"The view taken of a University in these Discourses is the
following:—that it is a place of *teaching* universal *knowledge*.
This implies that its object is, on the one hand, intellectual,
not moral; and, on the other, that it is the diffusion and exten-
sion of knowledge rather than the advancement. If its object
were scientific and philosophical discovery, I do not see why a
University should have students; if religious training, I do not
see how it can be the seat of literature and science.

"Such is a University in its *essence,* and independently of its
relation to the Church. But, practically speaking, it cannot 10
fulfil its object duly, such as I have described it, without the
Church's assistance; or, to use the theological term, the Church
is necessary for its *integrity*. Not that its main characters are
changed by this incorporation: it still has the office of intellectual education; but the Church steadies it in the performance
of that office."

DISCOURSE I

INTRODUCTORY

"The views to which I have referred have grown into my
whole system of thought, and are, as it were, part of myself.
Many changes has my mind gone through: here it has known
no variation or vacillation of opinion, and though this by itself 20

is no proof of the truth of my principles, it puts a seal upon conviction, and is a justification of earnestness and zeal. Those principles, which I am now to set forth under the sanction of the Catholic Church, were my profession at that early period of my life, when religion was to me more a matter of feeling and experience than of faith. They did but take greater hold upon me, as I was introduced to the records of Christian Antiquity, and approached in sentiment and desire to Catholicism; and my sense of their correctness has been increased with
30 the events of every year since I have been brought within its pale. . . . Let it be observed, then, that the principles on which I would conduct the inquiry are attainable, as I have already implied, by the mere experience of life. They do not come simply of theology; they imply no supernatural discernment; they have no special connexion with Revelation; they almost arise out of the nature of the case; they are dictated even by human prudence and wisdom, though a divine illumination be absent, and they are recognized by common sense, even where self-interest is not present to quicken it; and, therefore,
40 though true, and just, and good in themselves, they imply nothing whatever as to the religious profession of those who maintain them. They may be held by Protestants as well as by Catholics. . . . I have no intention, in any thing I shall say, of bringing into the argument the authority of the Church, or any authority at all; but I shall consider the question simply on the grounds of human reason and human wisdom. I am investigating in the abstract, and am determining what is in itself right and true."

DISCOURSE II

THEOLOGY A BRANCH OF KNOWLEDGE

"Religious doctrine is knowledge. This is the important
50 truth, little entered into at this day. . . . I am not catching at sharp arguments, but laying down grave principles. Religious

doctrine is knowledge, in as full a sense as Newton's doctrine is knowledge. University Teaching without Theology is simply unphilosophical. Theology has at least as good a right to claim a place there as Astronomy."

DISCOURSE III

BEARING OF THEOLOGY ON OTHER KNOWLEDGE

"If the various branches of knowledge, which are the matter of teaching in a University, so hang together, that none can be neglected without prejudice to the perfection of the rest, and if Theology be a branch of knowledge, of wide reception, of philosophical structure, of unutterable importance, and of 60 supreme influence, to what conclusion are we brought from these two premises but this? that to withdraw Theology from the public schools is to impair the completeness and to invalidate the trustworthiness of all that is actually taught in them. . . . In a word, Religious Truth is not only a portion, but a condition of general knowledge."

DISCOURSE IV

BEARING OF OTHER KNOWLEDGE ON THEOLOGY

"If you drop any science out of the circle of knowledge, you cannot keep its place vacant for it; that science is forgotten; the other sciences close up, or, in other words, they exceed their proper bounds, and intrude where they have no right. For 70 instance, I suppose, if ethics were sent into banishment, its territory would soon disappear, under a treaty of partition, as it may be called, between law, political economy, and physiology; what, again, would become of the province of experi-

mental science, if made over to the Antiquarian Society; or of history, if surrendered out and out to Metaphysicians? The case is the same with the subject-matter of Theology; it would be the prey of a dozen various sciences, if Theology were put out of possession; and not only so, but those sciences would be
80 plainly exceeding their rights and their capacities in seizing upon it. They would be sure to teach wrongly, where they had no mission to teach at all. .... The human mind cannot keep from speculating and systematizing; and if Theology is not allowed to occupy its own territory, adjacent sciences, nay, sciences which are quite foreign to Theology, will take possession of it. And this occupation is proved to be a usurpation by this circumstance, that these foreign sciences will assume certain principles as true, and act upon them, which they neither have authority to lay down themselves, nor appeal to
90 any other higher science to lay down for them."

DISCOURSE V

KNOWLEDGE ITS OWN END
(Reprinted here, as I)

DISCOURSE VI

KNOWLEDGE VIEWED IN RELATION TO LEARNING
(Reprinted here, as II)

DISCOURSE VII

KNOWLEDGE VIEWED IN RELATION TO PROFESSIONAL SKILL
(Reprinted here, as III)

DISCOURSE VIII

KNOWLEDGE VIEWED IN RELATION TO RELIGION

(Reprinted here, as IV)

DISCOURSE IX

DUTIES OF THE CHURCH TOWARDS KNOWLEDGE

"I have been ... inquiring what a University is, what is its aim, what its nature, what its bearings. I have accordingly laid down first, that all branches of knowledge are, at least implicitly, the subject-matter of its teaching; that these branches are not isolated and independent one of another, but form *95* together a whole or system; that they run into each other, and *to* complete each other, and that, in proportion to our view of *96* them as a whole, is the exactness and trustworthiness of the knowledge which they separately convey; that the process of imparting knowledge to the intellect in this philosophical way *100* is its true culture; that such culture is a good in itself; that the knowledge which is both its instrument and result is called Liberal Knowledge; that such culture, together with the knowledge which effects it, may fitly be sought for its own sake; that it is, however, in addition, of great secular utility, as constituting the best and highest formation of the intellect for social and political life; and lastly, that, considered in a religious aspect, it concurs with Christianity a certain way, and then diverges from it; and consequently proves in the event, sometimes its serviceable ally, sometimes, from its very resem- *110* blance to it, an insidious and dangerous foe. . . .

"Liberal Knowledge has a special tendency, not necessary or rightful, but a tendency in fact, when cultivated by beings

such as we are, to impress us with a mere philosophical theory of life and conduct, in the place of Revelation. . . . Truth has two attributes—beauty and power; and while Useful Knowledge is the possession of truth as powerful, Liberal Knowledge is the apprehension of it as beautiful. Pursue it, either as beauty or as power, to its furthest extent and its true limit, and
120 you are led by either road to the Eternal and Infinite, to the intimations of conscience and the announcements of the Church. Satisfy yourself with what is only visibly or intelligibly excellent, as you are likely to do, and you will make present utility and natural beauty the practical test of truth, and the sufficient object of the intellect. It is not that you will at once reject Catholicism, but you will measure and proportion it by an earthly standard. You will throw its highest and most momentous disclosures into the background, you will deny its principles, explain away its doctrines, re-arrange its
130 precepts, and make light of its practices, even while you profess it. Knowledge, viewed as Knowledge, exerts a subtle influence in throwing us back on ourselves, and making us our own centre, and our minds the measure of all things. This then is the tendency of that Liberal Education, of which a University is the school. . . .

"The book of nature is called Science, the book of man is called Literature. Literature and Science, thus considered, nearly constitute the subject-matter of Liberal Education. . . . Let her (the Church) do for Literature in one way what she
140 does for Science in another; each has its imperfection, and she has a remedy for each. She fears no knowledge, but she purifies all; she represses no element of our nature, but cultivates the whole. Science is grave, methodical, logical; with Science then she argues, and opposes reason to reason. Literature does not argue, but declaims and insinuates; it is multiform and versatile: it persuades instead of convincing, it seduces, it carries captive; it appeals to the sense of honour, or to the imagination, or to the stimulus of curiosity; it makes its way by means of gaiety, satire, romance, the beautiful, the pleasurable. Is it

wonderful that with an agent like this the Church should 150
claim to deal with a vigour corresponding to its restlessness, to
interfere in its proceedings with a higher hand, and to wield
an authority in the choice of its studies and of its books which
would be tyrannical, if reason and fact were the only instruments of its conclusions? But, anyhow, her principle is one and
the same throughout; not to prohibit truth of any kind, but to
see that no doctrines pass under the name of Truth but those
which claim it rightfully.

THE USES
OF KNOWLEDGE

I

KNOWLEDGE ITS OWN END

A university may be considered with reference either to its Students or to its Studies; and the principle, that all Knowledge is a whole and the separate Sciences parts of one, which I have hitherto been using in behalf of its studies, is equally important when we direct our attention to its students. Now then I turn to the students, and shall consider the education which, by virtue of this principle, a University will give them; and thus I shall be introduced, Gentlemen, to the second question, which I proposed to discuss, viz. whether and in what
10 sense its teaching, viewed relatively to the taught, carries the attribute of Utility along with it.

1

I have said that all branches of knowledge are connected together, because the subject-matter of knowledge is intimately united in itself, as being the acts and the work of the Creator. Hence it is that the Sciences, into which our knowl edge may be said to be cast, have multiplied bearings one on another, and an internal sympathy, and admit, or rather demand, comparison and adjustment. They complete, correct, balance each other. This consideration, if well-founded, must
20 be taken into account, not only as regards the attainment of truth, which is their common end, but as regards the influence

8

which they exercise upon those whose education consists in the study of them. I have said already, that to give undue prominence to one is to be unjust to another; to neglect or supersede these is to divert those from their proper object. It is to unsettle the boundary lines between science and science, to disturb their action, to destroy the harmony which binds them together. Such a proceeding will have a corresponding effect when introduced into a place of education. There is no science but tells a different tale, when viewed as a portion of a 30 whole, from what it is likely to suggest when taken by itself, without the safeguard, as I may call it, of others.

Let me make use of an illustration. In the combination of colours, very different effects are produced by a difference in their selection and juxta-position; red, green, and white change their shades, according to the contrast to which they are submitted. And, in like manner, the drift and meaning of a branch of knowledge varies with the company in which it is introduced to the student. If his reading is confined simply to one subject, however such division of labour may favour 40 the advancement of a particular pursuit, a point into which I do not here enter, certainly it has a tendency to contract his mind. If it is incorporated with others, it depends on those others as to the kind of influence which it exerts upon him. Thus the Classics, which in England are the means of refining the taste, have in France subserved the spread of revolutionary and deistical doctrines. In Metaphysics, again, Butler's *Analogy of Religion,* which has had so much to do with the conversion to the Catholic faith of members of the University of Oxford, appeared to Pitt and others, who had received a 50 different training, to operate only in the direction of infidelity. And so again, Watson, Bishop of Llandaff, as I think he tells us in the narrative of his life, felt the science of Mathematics to indispose the mind to religious belief, while others see in its investigations the best parallel, and thereby defence, of the Christian Mysteries. In like manner, I suppose, Arcesilas would not have handled logic as Aristotle, nor Aristotle have criticized poets as Plato; yet reasoning and poetry are subject to scientific rules.

60   It is a great point then to enlarge the range of studies which a University professes, even for the sake of the students; and, though they cannot pursue every subject which is open to them, they will be the gainers by living among those and under those who represent the whole circle. This I conceive to be the advantage of a seat of universal learning, considered as a place of education. An assemblage of learned men, zealous for their own sciences, and rivals of each other, are brought, by familiar intercourse and for the sake of intellectual peace, to adjust together the claims and relations of their respective

70   subjects of investigation. They learn to respect, to consult, to aid each other. Thus is created a pure and clear atmosphere of thought, which the student also breathes, though in his own case he only pursues a few sciences out of the multitude. He profits by an intellectual tradition, which is independent of particular teachers, which guides him in his choice of subjects, and duly interprets for him those which he chooses. He apprehends the great outlines of knowledge, the principles on which it rests, the scale of its parts, its lights and its shades, its great points and its little, as he otherwise cannot apprehend them.

80   Hence it is that his education is called "Liberal." A habit of mind is formed which lasts through life, of which the attributes are, freedom, equitableness, calmness, moderation, and wisdom; or what in a former Discourse I have ventured to call a philosophical habit. This then I would assign as the special fruit of the education furnished at a University, as contrasted with other places of teaching or modes of teaching. This is the main purpose of a University in its treatment of its students.

And now the question is asked me, What is the *use* of it? and my answer will constitute the main subject of the Dis-

90   courses which are to follow.

2

Cautious and practical thinkers, I say, will ask me, what, after all, is the gain of this Philosophy, of which I make such account, and from which I promise so much. Even supposing it to enable us to exercise the degree of trust exactly due to every science respectively, and to estimate precisely the value of every truth which is anywhere to be found, how are we better for this master view of things, which I have been extolling? Does it not reverse the principle of the division of labour? will practical objects be obtained better or worse by its cultivation? to what then does it lead? where does it end? what does it do? how does it profit? what does it promise? Particular sciences are respectively the basis of definite arts, which carry on to results tangible and beneficial the truths which are the subjects of the knowledge attained; what is the Art of this science of sciences? what is the fruit of such a Philosophy? what are we proposing to effect, what inducements do we hold out to the Catholic community, when we set about the enterprise of founding a University?

I am asked what is the end of University Education, and of the Liberal or Philosophical Knowledge which I conceive it to impart: I answer, that what I have already said has been sufficient to show that it has a very tangible, real, and sufficient end, though the end cannot be divided from that knowledge itself. Knowledge is capable of being its own end. Such is the constitution of the human mind, that any kind of knowledge, if it be really such, is its own reward. And if this is true of all knowledge, it is true also of that special Philosophy, which I have made to consist in a comprehensive view of truth in all its branches, of the relations of science to science, of their mutual bearings, and their respective values. What the worth of such an acquirement is, compared with other objects which we seek,—wealth or power or honour or the conveniences and comforts of life, I do not profess here to discuss; but I would maintain, and mean to show, that it is an object, in its own nature so really and undeniably good, as to be the compensation of a great deal of thought in the compassing, and a great deal of trouble in the attaining.

Now, when I say that Knowledge is, not merely a means to something beyond it, or the preliminary of certain arts into 130 which it naturally resolves, but an end sufficient to rest in and to pursue for its own sake, surely I am uttering no paradox, for I am stating what is both intelligible in itself, and has ever been the common judgment of philosophers and the ordinary feeling of mankind. I am saying what at least the public opinion of this day ought to be slow to deny, considering how much we have heard of late years, in opposition to Religion, of entertaining, curious, and various knowledge. I am but saying what whole volumes have been written to illustrate, viz., by a "selection from the records of Philosophy, Literature, and 140 Art, in all ages and countries, of a body of examples, to show how the most unpropitious circumstances have been unable to conquer an ardent desire for the acquisition of knowledge." [1] That further advantages accrue to us and redound to others by its possession, over and above what it is in itself, I am very far indeed from denying; but, independent of these, we are satisfying a direct need of our nature in its very acquisition; and, whereas our nature, unlike that of the inferior creation, does not at once reach its perfection, but depends, in order to it, on a number of external aids and appliances, Knowledge, as 150 one of the principal of these, is valuable for what its very presence in us does for us after the manner of a habit, even though it be turned to no further account, nor subserve any direct end.

3

Hence it is that Cicero, in enumerating the various heads of mental excellence, lays down the pursuit of Knowledge for its own sake, as the first of them. "This pertains most of all to

1. "Pursuit of Knowledge under Difficulties." Introd. By George Lillie Craik.   2. Cicero. *De Officiis, Initium.*

human nature," he says, "for we are all of us drawn to the pursuit of Knowledge; in which to excel we consider excellent, whereas to mistake, to err, to be ignorant, to be deceived, is both an evil and a disgrace." [2] And he considers Knowledge the very first object to which we are attracted, after the supply of our physical wants. After the calls and duties of our animal existence, as they may be termed, as regards ourselves, our family, and our neighbours, follows, he tells us, "the search after truth. Accordingly, as soon we escape from the pressure of necessary cares, forthwith we desire to see, to hear, and to learn; and consider the knowledge of what is hidden or is wonderful a condition of our happiness."

This passage, though it is but one of many similar passages in a multitude of authors, I take for the very reason that it is so familiarly known to us; and I wish you to observe, Gentlemen, how distinctly it separates the pursuit of Knowledge from those ulterior objects to which certainly it can be made to conduce, and which are, I suppose, solely contemplated by the persons who would ask of me the use of a University or Liberal Education. So far from dreaming of the cultivation of Knowledge directly and mainly in order to our physical comfort and enjoyment, for the sake of life and person, of health, of the conjugal and family union, of the social tie and civil security, the great Orator implies, that it is only after our physical and political needs are supplied, and when we are "free from necessary duties and cares," that we are in a condition for "desiring to see, to hear, and to learn." Nor does he contemplate in the least degree the reflex or subsequent action of Knowledge, when acquired, upon those material goods which we set out by securing before we seek it; on the contrary, he expressly denies its bearing upon social life altogether, strange as such a procedure is to those who live after the rise of the Baconian philosophy, and he cautions us against such a cultivation of it as will interfere with our duties to our fellow-creatures. "All these methods," he says, "are engaged in the investigation of truth; by the pursuit of which to be carried off from public occupations is a transgression of duty. For the praise of virtue lies altogether in action; yet intermissions often occur, and then we recur to such pursuits; not to say that the incessant activity of the mind is vigorous enough to carry us on in the pursuit of knowledge, even without any exertion of our own." The idea of benefiting society by means of "the pursuit of science and knowledge" did not enter at all into the motives which he would assign for their cultivation.

200   This was the ground of the opposition which the elder Cato made to the introduction of Greek Philosophy among his countrymen, when Carneades and his companions, on occasion of their embassy, were charming the Roman youth with their eloquent expositions of it. The fit representative of a practical people, Cato estimated every thing by what it produced; whereas the Pursuit of Knowledge promised nothing beyond Knowledge itself. He despised that refinement or enlargement of mind of which he had no experience.

4

Things, which can bear to be cut off from every thing else
210 and yet persist in living, must have life in themselves; pursuits, which issue in nothing, and still maintain their ground for ages, which are regarded as admirable, though they have not as yet proved themselves to be useful, must have their sufficient end in themselves, whatever it turn out to be. And we are brought to the same conclusion by considering the force of the epithet, by which the knowledge under consideration is popularly designated. It is common to speak of "*liberal* knowledge," of the "*liberal* arts and studies," and of a "*liberal* education," as the especial characteristic or property of a Uni-
220 versity and of a gentleman; what is really meant by the word? Now, first, in its grammatical sense it is opposed to *servile;* and by "servile work" is understood, as our catechisms inform us, bodily labour, mechanical employment, and the like, in which the mind has little or no part. Parallel to such servile

works are those arts, if they deserve the name, of which the
poet speaks,[3] which owe their origin and their method to
hazard, not to skill; as, for instance, the practice and operation
of an empiric. As far as this contrast may be considered as a
guide into the meaning of the word, liberal education and
liberal pursuits are exercises of mind, of reason, of reflection.   230

But we want something more for its explanation, for there
are bodily exercises which are liberal, and mental exercises
which are not so. For instance, in ancient times the practitioners in medicine were commonly slaves; yet it was an art as
intellectual in its nature, in spite of the pretence, fraud, and
quackery with which it might then, as now, be debased, as it
was heavenly in its aim. And so in like manner, we contrast
a liberal education with a commercial education or a professional; yet no one can deny that commerce and the professions
afford scope for the highest and most diversified powers of   240
mind. There is then a great variety of intellectual exercises,
which are not technically called "liberal;" on the other hand,
I say, there are exercises of the body which do receive that appellation. Such, for instance, was the palæstra, in ancient
times; such the Olympic games, in which strength and dexterity of body as well as of mind gained the prize. In Xenophon
we read of the young Persian nobility being taught to ride on
horseback and to speak the truth; both being among the accomplishments of a gentleman. War, too, however rough a
profession, has ever been accounted liberal, unless in cases   250
when it becomes heroic, which would introduce us to another
subject.

Now comparing these instances together, we shall have no
difficulty in determining the principle of this apparent variation in the application of the term which I am examining.
Manly games, or games of skill, or military prowess, though
bodily, are, it seems, accounted liberal; on the other hand,
what is merely professional, though highly intellectual, nay,

3. Art loves fate and fate loves art. Aristotle, *Nicomachean Ethics,* vi.

though liberal in comparison of trade and manual labour, is
260 not simply called liberal, and mercantile occupations are not
liberal at all. Why this distinction? because that alone is liberal
knowledge, which stands on its own pretensions, which is independent of sequel, expects no complement, refuses to be
informed (as it is called) by any end, or absorbed into any
art, in order duly to present itself to our contemplation. The
most ordinary pursuits have this specific character, if they are
self-sufficient and complete; the highest lose it, when they
minister to something beyond them. It is absurd to balance,
in point of worth and importance, a treatise on reducing frac-
270 tures with a game of cricket or a fox-chase; yet of the two the
bodily exercise has that quality which we call "liberal," and
the intellectual has it not. And so of the learned professions
altogether, considered merely as professions; although one of
them be the most popularly beneficial, and another the most
politically important, and the third the most intimately divine
of all human pursuits, yet the very greatness of their end, the
health of the body, or of the commonwealth, or of the soul,
diminishes, not increases, their claim to the appellation "liberal," and that still more, if they are cut down to the strict
280 exigencies of that end. If, for instance, Theology, instead of
being cultivated as a contemplation, be limited to the purposes
of the pulpit or be represented by the catechism, it loses,—
not its usefulness, not its divine character, not its meritorious-
ness (rather it gains a claim upon these titles by such charit-
able condescension),—but it does lose the particular attribute
which I am illustrating; just as a face worn by tears and fast-
ing loses its beauty, or a labourer's hand loses its delicateness;
—for Theology thus exercised is not simple knowledge, but
rather is an art or a business making use of Theology. And
290 thus it appears that even what is supernatural need not be
liberal, nor need a hero be a gentleman, for the plain reason
that one idea is not another idea. And in like manner the
Baconian Philosophy, by using its physical sciences in the
service of man, does thereby transfer them from the order of

Liberal Pursuits to, I do not say the inferior, but the distinct class of the Useful. And, to take a different instance, hence again, as is evident, whenever personal gain is the motive, still more distinctive an effect has it upon the character of a given pursuit; thus racing, which was a liberal exercise in Greece, forfeits its rank in times like these, so far as it is made the 300 occasion of gambling.

All that I have been now saying is summed up in a few characteristic words of the great Philosopher. "Of possessions," he says, "those rather are useful, which bear fruit; those *liberal, which tend to enjoyment.* By fruitful, I mean, which yield revenue; by enjoyable, where *nothing accrues of consequence beyond the using."* [4]

5

Do not suppose, that in thus appealing to the ancients, I am throwing back the world two thousand years, and fettering Philosophy with the reasonings of paganism. While the 310 world lasts, will Aristotle's doctrine on these matters last, for he is the oracle of nature and of truth. While we are men, we cannot help, to a great extent, being Aristotelians, for the great Master does but analyze the thoughts, feelings, views, and opinions of human kind. He has told us the meaning of our own words and ideas, before we were born. In many subject-matters, to think correctly, is to think like Aristotle; and we are his disciples whether we will or no, though we may not know it. Now, as to the particular instance before us, the word "liberal" as applied to Knowledge and Education, expresses a 320 specific idea, which ever has been, and ever will be, while the nature of man is the same, just as the idea of the Beautiful is specific, or of the Sublime, or of the Ridiculous, or of the Sordid. It is in the world now, it was in the world then; and, as in the case of the dogmas of faith, it is illustrated by a continuous historical tradition, and never was out of the world,

4. Aristotle, *Rhetoric,* i, 5.

from the time it came into it. There have indeed been differences of opinion from time to time, as to what pursuits and what arts came under that idea, but such differences are but
330 an additional evidence of its reality. That idea must have a substance in it, which has maintained its ground amid these conflicts and changes, which has ever served as a standard to measure things withal, which has passed from mind to mind unchanged, when there was so much to colour, so much to influence any notion or thought whatever, which was not founded in our very nature. Were it a mere generalization, it would have varied with the subjects from which it was generalized; but though its subjects vary with the age, it varies not itself. The palæstra may seem a liberal exercise to Lycurgus,
340 and illiberal to Seneca; coach-driving and prize-fighting may be recognized in Elis, and be condemned in England; music may be despicable in the eyes of certain moderns, and be in the highest place with Aristotle and Plato,—(and the case is the same in the particular application of the idea of Beauty, or of Goodness, or of Moral Virtue, there is a difference of tastes, a difference of judgments)—still these variations imply, instead of discrediting, the archetypal idea, which is but a previous hypothesis or condition, by means of which issue is joined between contending opinions, and without which there would
350 be nothing to dispute about.

I consider, then, that I am chargeable with no paradox, when I speak of a Knowledge which is its own end, when I call it liberal knowledge, or a gentleman's knowledge, when I educate for it, and make it the scope of a University. And still less am I incurring such a charge, when I make this acquisition consist, not in Knowledge in a vague and ordinary sense, but in that Knowledge which I have especially called Philosophy or, in an extended sense of the word, Science; for whatever claims Knowledge has to be considered as a good, these
360 it has in a higher degree when it is viewed not vaguely, not popularly, but precisely and transcendently as Philosophy. Knowledge, I say, is then especially liberal, or sufficient for

itself, apart from every external and ulterior object, when and so far as it is philosophical, and this I proceed to show.

6

Now bear with me, Gentlemen, if what I am about to say, has at first sight a fanciful appearance. Philosophy, then, or Science, is related to Knowledge in this way:—Knowledge is called by the name of Science or Philosophy, when it is acted upon, informed, or if I may use a strong figure, impregnated by Reason. Reason is the principle of that intrinsic fecundity 370 of Knowledge, which, to those who possess it, is its especial value, and which dispenses with the necessity of their looking abroad for any end to rest upon external to itself. Knowledge, indeed, when thus exalted into a scientific form, is also power; not only is it excellent in itself, but whatever such excellence may be, it is something more, it has a result beyond itself. Doubtless; but that is a further consideration, with which I am not concerned. I only say that, prior to its being a power, it is a good; that it is, not only an instrument, but an end. I know well it may resolve itself into an art, and terminate in a me- 380 chanical process, and in tangible fruit; but it also may fall back upon that Reason which informs it, and resolve itself into Philosophy. In one case it is called Useful Knowledge, in the other Liberal. The same person may cultivate it in both ways at once; but this again is a matter foreign to my subject; here I do but say that there are two ways of using Knowledge, and in matter of fact those who use it in one way are not likely to use it in the other, or at least in a very limited measure. You see, then, here are two methods of Education; the end of the one is to be philosophical, of the other to be mechanical; the 390 one rises towards general ideas, the other is exhausted upon what is particular and external. Let me not be thought to deny the necessity, or to decry the benefit, of such attention to what is particular and practical, as belongs to the useful or mechanical arts; life could not go on without them; we owe our daily welfare to them; their exercise is the duty of the many, and we owe to the many a debt of gratitude for fulfilling that duty. I only say that Knowledge, in proportion as it tends more and more to be particular, ceases to be Knowledge. It is a question whether Knowledge can in any proper sense be predicated of the brute creation; without pretending to metaphysical exactness of phraseology, which would be unsuitable to an occasion like this, I say, it seems to me improper to call that passive sensation, or perception of things, which brutes seem to possess, by the name of Knowledge. When I speak of Knowledge, I mean something intellectual, something which grasps what it perceives through the senses; something which takes a view of things; which sees more than the senses convey; which reasons upon what it sees, and while it sees; which invests it with an idea. It expresses itself, not in a mere enunciation, but by an enthymeme: it is of the nature of science from the first, and in this consists its dignity. The principle of real dignity in Knowledge, its worth, its desirableness, considered irrespectively of its results, is this germ within it of a scientific or a philosophical process. This is how it comes to be an end in itself; this is why it admits of being called Liberal. Not to know the relative disposition of things is the state of slaves or children; to have mapped out the Universe is the boast, or at least the ambition, of Philosophy.

Moreover, such knowledge is not a mere extrinsic or accidental advantage, which is ours to-day and anothers' to-morrow, which may be got up from a book, and easily forgotten again, which we can command or communicate at our pleasure, which we can borrow for the occasion, carry about in our hand, and take into the market; it is an acquired illumination, it is a habit, a personal possession, and an inward endowment. And this is the reason, why it is more correct, as well as more usual, to speak of a University as a place of education, than of instruction, though, when knowledge is concerned, instruction would at first sight have seemed the more appropriate word. We are instructed, for instance, in manual exercises, in

the fine and useful arts, in trades, and in ways of busine
these are methods, which have little or no effect up
mind itself, are contained in rules committed to memory, to
tradition, or to use, and bear upon an end external to themselves. But education is a higher word; it implies an action
upon our mental nature, and the formation of a character; it is
something individual and permanent, and is commonly
spoken of in connexion with religion and virtue. When, then,
we speak of the communication of Knowledge as being Edu-   440
cation, we thereby really imply that that Knowledge is a state
or condition of mind; and since cultivation of mind is surely
worth seeking for its own sake, we are thus brought once more
to the conclusion, which the word "Liberal" and the word
"Philosophy" have already suggested, that there is a Knowl-   445
edge, which is desirable, though nothing come of it, as being
of itself a treasure, and a sufficient remuneration of years of
labour.

7

This, then, is the answer which I am prepared to give to
the question with which I opened this Discourse. Before go-   450
ing on to speak of the object of the Church in taking up
Philosophy, and the uses to which she puts it, I am prepared
to maintain that Philosophy is its own end, and, as I conceive,
I have now begun the proof of it. I am prepared to maintain
that there is a knowledge worth possessing for what it is, and
not merely for what it does; and what minutes remain to me
to-day I shall devote to the removal of some portion of the
indistinctness and confusion with which the subject may in
some minds be surrounded.

It may be objected then, that, when we profess to seek   460
Knowledge for some end or other beyond itself, whatever it
be, we speak intelligibly; but that, whatever men may have
said, however obstinately the idea may have kept its ground
from age to age, still it is simply unmeaning to say that we
seek Knowledge for its own sake, and for nothing else; for that

it ever leads to something beyond itself, which therefore is its end, and the cause why it is desirable;—moreover, that this end is twofold, either of this world or of the next; that all knowledge is cultivated either for secular objects or for eternal; that if it is directed to secular objects, it is called Useful Knowledge, if to eternal, Religious or Christian Knowledge;—in consequence, that if, as I have allowed, this Liberal Knowledge does not benefit the body or estate, it ought to benefit the soul; but if the fact be really so, that it is neither a physical or a secular good on the one hand, nor a moral good on the other, it cannot be a good at all, and is not worth the trouble which is necessary for its acquisition.

And then I may be reminded that the professors of this Liberal or Philosophical Knowledge have themselves, in every age, recognized this exposition of the matter, and have submitted to the issue in which it terminates; for they have ever been attempting to make men virtuous; or, if not, at least have assumed that refinement of mind was virtue, and that they themselves were the virtuous portion of mankind. This they have professed on the one hand; and on the other, they have utterly failed in their professions, so as ever to make themselves a proverb among men, and a laughing-stock both to the grave and the dissipated portion of mankind, in consequence of them. Thus they have furnished against themselves both the ground and the means of their own exposure, without any trouble at all to any one else. In a word, from the time that Athens was the University of the world, what has Philosophy taught men, but to promise without practising, and to aspire without attaining? What has the deep and lofty thought of its disciples ended in but eloquent words? Nay, what has its teaching ever meditated, when it was boldest in its remedies for human ill, beyond charming us to sleep by its lessons, that we might feel nothing at all? like some melodious air, or rather like those strong and transporting perfumes, which at first spread their sweetness over every thing they touch, but in a little while do but offend in proportion as they once pleased us. Did Philosophy support Cicero under the disfavour of the fickle populace, or nerve Seneca to oppose an imperial tyrant? It abandoned Brutus, as he sorrowfully confessed, in his greatest need, and it forced Cato, as his panegyrist strangely boasts, into the false position of defying heaven. How few can be counted among its professors, who, like Polemo, were thereby converted from a profligate course, or like Anaxagoras, thought the world well lost in exchange for its possession? The philosopher in *Rasselas* [5] taught a superhuman doctrine, and then succumbed without an effort to a trial of human affection. 510

"He discoursed," we are told, "with great energy on the government of the passions. His look was venerable, his action graceful, his pronunciation clear, and his diction elegant. He showed, with great strength of sentiment and variety of illustration, that human nature is degraded and debased, when the lower faculties predominate over the higher. He communicated the various precepts given, from time to time, for the conquest of passion, and displayed the happiness of those who had obtained the important victory, after which man is no 520 longer the slave of fear, nor the fool of hope . . . He enumerated many examples of heroes immoveable by pain or pleasure, who looked with indifference on those modes or accidents to which the vulgar give the names of good and evil."

Rasselas in a few days found the philosopher in a room half darkened, with his eyes misty, and his face pale. "Sir," said he, "you have come at a time when all human friendship is useless; what I suffer cannot be remedied, what I have lost cannot be supplied. My daughter, my only daughter, from whose tenderness I expected all the comforts of my age, died 530 last night of a fever." "Sir," said the prince, "mortality is an event by which a wise man can never be surprised; we know that death is always near, and it should therefore always be expected." "Young man," answered the philosopher, "you speak like one who has never felt the pangs of separation."

5. A philosophical novel, by Samuel Johnson.

"Have you, then, forgot the precept," said Rasselas, "which you so powerfully enforced? . . . consider that external things are naturally variable, but truth and reason are always the same." "What comfort," said the mourner, "can truth and
540 reason afford me? Of what effect are they now, but to tell me that my daughter will not be restored?"

8

Better, far better, to make no professions, you will say, than to·cheat others with what we are not, and to scandalize them with what we are. The sensualist, or the man of the world, at any rate is not the victim of fine words, but pursues a reality and gains it. The Philosophy of Utility, you will say, Gentlemen, has at least done its work; and I grant it,—it aimed low, but it has fulfilled its aim. If that man of great intellect who has been its Prophet [6] in the conduct of life played false to his
550 own professions, he was not bound by his philosophy to be true to his friend or faithful in his trust. Moral virtue was not the line in which he undertook to instruct men; and though, as the poet [7] calls him, he were the "meanest" of mankind, he was so in what may be called his private capacity and without any prejudice to the theory of induction. He had a right to be so, if he chose, for any thing that the Idols [8] of the den or the theatre had to say to the contrary. His mission was the increase of physical enjoyment and social comfort; [9] and most wonderfully, most awfully has he fulfilled his conception and his
560 design. Almost day by day have we fresh and fresh shoots, and buds, and blossoms, which are to ripen into fruit, on that magical tree of Knowledge which he planted, and to which none of us perhaps, except the very poor, but owes, if not his present life, at least his daily food, his health, and general well-being.

6. Francis Bacon. 7. Alexander Pope, "An Essay on Man," iv.
8. Bacon, *Novum Organum,* vi, 553. 9. [Newman's note: It will be seen that on the whole I agree with Lord Macaulay in his Essay on Bacon's Philosophy. I do not know whether he would agree with me.]

He was the divinely provided minister of temporal benefits to all of us so great, that, whatever I am forced to think of him as a man, I have not the heart, from mere gratitude, to speak of him severely. And, in spite of the tendencies of his philosophy, which are, as we see at this day, to depreciate, or to trample on Theology, he has himself, in his writings, gone out of his way, as if with a prophetic misgiving of those tendencies, to insist on it as the instrument of that beneficent Father,[10] who, when He came on earth in visible form, took on Him first and most prominently the office of assuaging the bodily wounds of human nature. And truly, like the old mediciner in the tale, "he sat diligently at his work, and hummed, with cheerful countenance, a pious song;" and then in turn "went out singing into the meadows so gaily, that those who had seen him from afar might well have thought it was a youth gathering flowers for his beloved, instead of an old physician gathering healing herbs in the morning dew." [11]

Alas, that men, in the action of life or in their heart of hearts, are not what they seem to be in their moments of excitement, or in their trances or intoxications of genius,—so good, so noble, so serene! Alas, that Bacon too in his own way should after all be but the fellow of those heathen philosophers who in their disadvantages had some excuse for their inconsistency, and who surprise us rather in what they did say than in what they did not do! Alas, that he too, like Socrates or Seneca, must be stripped of his holy-day coat, which looks so fair, and should be but a mockery amid his most majestic gravity of phrase; and, for all his vast abilities, should, in the littleness of his own moral being, but typify the intellectual narrowness of his school! However, granting all this, heroism after all was not his philosophy:—I cannot deny he has abundantly achieved what he proposed. His is simply a Method whereby bodily discomforts and temporal wants are to be most effectually removed from the greatest number; and already, before it has

10. Bacon, *De Augmentis Scientiarum,* iv. 2; Macaulay, "Lord Bacon"; Bacon, *Praef. Instauratio Magna.* 11. Fouque's *Unknown Patient.*

shown any signs of exhaustion, the gifts of nature, in their
600 most artificial shapes and luxurious profusion and diversity,
from all quarters of the earth, are, it is undeniable, by its
means brought even to our doors, and we rejoice in them.

9

Useful Knowledge then, I grant, has done its work; and
Liberal Knowledge as certainly has not done its work,—that
is, supposing, as the objectors assume, its direct end, like Religious Knowledge, is to make men better; but this I will not
for an instant allow, and, unless I allow it, those objectors have
said nothing to the purpose. I admit, rather I maintain, what
they have been urging, for I consider Knowledge to have its
610 end in itself. For all its friends, or its enemies, may say, I insist
upon it, that it is as real a mistake to burden it with virtue or
religion as with the mechanical arts. Its direct business is not
to steel the soul against temptation or to console it in affliction,
any more than to set the loom in motion, or to direct the
steam carriage; be it ever so much the means or the condition
of both material and moral advancement, still, taken by and in
itself, it as little mends our hearts as it improves our temporal
circumstances. And if its eulogists claim for it such a power,
they commit the very same kind of encroachment on a prov-
620 ince not their own as the political economist who should
maintain that his science educated him for casuistry or diplo-
macy. Knowledge is one thing, virtue is another; good sense
is not conscience, refinement is not humility, nor is largeness
and justness of view faith. Philosophy, however enlightened,
however profound, gives no command over the passions, no
influential motives, no vivifying principles. Liberal Education
makes not the Christian, not the Catholic, but the gentleman.
It is well to be a gentleman, it is well to have a cultivated intellect, a delicate taste, a candid, equitable, dispassionate mind, a
630 noble and courteous bearing in the conduct of life;—these are
the connatural qualities of a large knowledge; they are the

objects of a University; I am advocating, I shall illustrate and insist upon them; but still, I repeat, they are no guarantee for sanctity or even for conscientiousness, they may attach to the man of the world, to the profligate, to the heartless,—pleasant, alas, and attractive as he shows when decked out in them. Taken by themselves, they do but seem to be what they are not; they look like virtue at a distance, but they are detected by close observers, and on the long run; and hence it is that they are popularly accused of pretence and hypocrisy, not, I 640 repeat, from their own fault, but because their professors and their admirers persist in taking them for what they are not, and are officious in arrogating for them a praise to which they have no claim. Quarry the granite rock with razors, or moor the vessel with a thread of silk; then may you hope with such keen and delicate instruments as human knowledge and human reason to contend against those giants, the passion and the pride of man.

Surely we are not driven to theories of this kind, in order to vindicate the value and dignity of Liberal Knowledge. Surely 650 the real grounds on which its pretensions rest are not so very subtle or abstruse, so very strange or improbable. Surely it is very intelligible to say, and that is what I say here, that Liberal Education, viewed in itself, is simply the cultivation of the intellect, as such, and its object is nothing more or less than intellectual excellence. Every thing has its own perfection, be it higher or lower in the scale of things; and the perfection of one is not the perfection of another. Things animate, inanimate, visible, invisible, all are good in their kind, and have a *best* of themselves, which is an object of pursuit. Why do you 660 take such pains with your garden or your park? You see to your walks and turf and shrubberies; to your trees and drives; not as if you meant to make an orchard of the one, or corn or pasture land of the other, but because there is a special beauty in all that is goodly in wood, water, plain, and slope, brought all together by art into one shape, and grouped into one whole. Your cities are beautiful, your palaces, your public buildings,

your territorial mansions, your churches; and their beauty leads to nothing beyond itself. There is a physical beauty and a
670 moral: there is a beauty of person, there is a beauty of our moral being, which is natural virtue; and in like manner there is a beauty, there is a perfection, of the intellect. There is an ideal perfection in these various subject-matters, towards which individual instances are seen to rise, and which are the standards for all instances whatever. The Greek divinities and demigods, as the statuary has moulded them, with their symmetry of figure, and their high forehead and their regular features, are the perfection of physical beauty. The heroes, of whom history tells, Alexander,
680 or Cæsar, or Scipio, or Saladin, are the representatives of that magnanimity or self-mastery which is the greatness of human nature. Christianity too has its heroes, and in the supernatural order, and we call them Saints. The artist puts before him beauty of feature and form; the poet, beauty of mind; the preacher, the beauty of grace: then intellect too, I repeat, has its beauty, and it has those who aim at it. To open the mind, to correct it, to refine it, to enable it to know, and to digest, master, rule, and use its knowledge, to give it power over its own faculties, application, flexibility, method, critical
690 exactness, sagacity, resource, address, eloquent expression, is an object as intelligible (for here we are inquiring, not what the object of a Liberal Education is worth, nor what use the Church makes of it, but what it is in itself), I say, an object as intelligible as the cultivation of virtue, while, at the same time, it is absolutely distinct from it.

10

This indeed is but a temporal object, and a transitory possession; but so are other things in themselves which we make much of and pursue. The moralist will tell us that man, in all his functions, is but a flower which blossoms and fades, except
700 so far as a higher principle breathes upon him, and makes him

and what he is immortal. Body and mind are carried on into an eternal state of being by the gifts of Divine Munificence; but at first they do but fail in a failing world; and if the powers of intellect decay, the powers of the body have decayed before them, and, as an Hospital or an Almshouse, though its end be ephemeral, may be sanctified to the service of religion, so surely may a University, even were it nothing more than I have as yet described it. We attain to heaven by using this world well, though it is to pass away; we perfect our nature, not by undoing it, but by adding to it what is more than   710 nature, and directing it towards aims higher than its own.

II

KNOWLEDGE VIEWED IN RELATION TO LEARNING

I

It were well if the English, like the Greek language, possessed some definite word to express, simply and generally, intellectual proficiency or perfection, such as "health," as used with reference to the animal frame, and "virtue," with reference to our moral nature. I am not able to find such a term;— talent, ability, genius, belong distinctly to the raw material, which is the subject-matter, not to that excellence which is the result of excercise and training. When we turn, indeed, to the particular kinds of intellectual perfection, words are forthcoming for our purpose, as, for instance, judgment, taste, and skill;   10 yet even these belong, for the most part, to powers or habits bearing upon practice or upon art, and not to any perfect condition of the intellect, considered in itself. Wisdom, again, is certainly a more comprehensive word than any other, but it

has a direct relation to conduct, and to human life. Knowledge, indeed, and Science express purely intellectual ideas, but still not a state or quality of the intellect; for knowledge, in its ordinary sense, is but one of its circumstances, denoting a possession or a habit; and science has been appropriated to the
20 subject-matter of the intellect, instead of belonging in English, as it ought to do, to the intellect itself. The consequence is that, on an occasion like this, many words are necessary, in order, first, to bring out and convey what surely is no difficult idea in itself,—that of the cultivation of the intellect as an end; next, in order to recommend what surely is no unreasonable object; and lastly, to describe and make the mind realize the particular perfection in which that object consists. Every one knows practically what are the constituents of health or virtue; and every one recognizes health and virtue as ends to be pursued; it is
30 otherwise with intellectual excellence, and this must be my excuse, if I seem to any one to be bestowing a good deal of labour on a preliminary matter.

In default of a recognized term, I have called the perfection or virtue of the intellect by the name of philosophy, philosophical knowledge, enlargement of mind, or illumination; terms which are not commonly given to it by writers of this day: but, whatever name we bestow on it, it is, I believe, as a matter of history, the business of a University to make this intellectual culture its direct scope, or to employ itself in the education of
40 the intellect,—just as the work of a Hospital lies in healing the sick or wounded, of a Riding or Fencing School, or of a Gymnasium, in exercising the limbs, of an Almshouse, in aiding and solacing the old, of an Orphanage, in protecting innocence, of a Penitentiary, in restoring the guilty. I say, a University, taken in its bare idea, and before we view it as an instrument of the Church, has this object and this mission; it contemplates neither moral impression nor mechanical production; it professes to exercise the mind neither in art nor in duty; its function is intellectual culture; here it may leave its
50 scholars, and it has done its work when it has done as much

as this. It educates the intellect to reason well in all matters, 1
reach out towards truth, and to grasp it.

2

This, I said in my foregoing Discourse, was the object of a 5̷3̷
University, viewed in itself, and apart from the Catholic
Church, or from the State, or from any other power which
may use it; and I illustrated this in various ways. I said that 5̷4̷
the intellect must have an excellence of its own, for there was
nothing which had not its specific good; that the word "educate" would not be used of intellectual culture, as it is used,
had not the intellect had an end of its own; that, had it not 60
such an end, there would be no meaning in calling certain
intellectual exercises "liberal," in contrast with "useful," as is
commonly done; that the very notion of a philosophical tem-
per implied it, for it threw us back upon research and system
as ends in themselves, distinct from effects and works of any
kind; that a philosophical scheme of knowledge, or system of
sciences, could not, from the nature of the case, issue in any
one definite art or pursuit, as its end; and that, on the other
hand, the discovery and contemplation of truth, to which research and systematizing led, were surely sufficient ends, 70
though nothing beyond them were added, and that they had
ever been accounted sufficient by mankind.

Here then I take up the subject; and, having determined
that the cultivation of the intellect is an end distinct and sufficient in itself, and that, so far as words go it is an enlargement or illumination, I proceed to inquire what this mental
breadth, or power, or light, or philosophy consists in. A Hospital heals a broken limb or cures a fever: what does an Institution effect, which professes the health, not of the body, not of
the soul, but of the intellect? What is this good, which in 80
former times, as well as our own, has been found worth the
notice, the appropriation, of the Catholic Church?

I have then to investigate, in the Discourses which follow,

those qualities and characteristics of the intellect in which its cultivation issues or rather consists; and, with a view of assisting myself in this undertaking, I shall recur to certain questions which have already been touched upon. These questions are three: viz. the relation of intellectual culture, first, to *mere* knowledge; secondly, to *professional* knowledge; and thirdly, 90 to *religious* knowledge. In other words, are *acquirements* and *attainments* the scope of a University Education? or *expertness in particular arts and pursuits?* or *moral and religious proficiency?* or something besides these three? These questions I shall examine in succession, with the purpose I have mentioned; and I hope to be excused, if, in this anxious undertaking, I am led to repeat what, either in these Discourses or elsewhere,[1] I have already put upon paper. And first, of *Mere Knowledge,* or Learning, and its connexion with intellectual illumination or Philosophy.

3

100   I suppose the *primâ-facie* view which the public at large would take of a University, considering it as a place of Education, is nothing more or less than a place for acquiring a great deal of knowledge on a great many subjects. Memory is one of the first developed of the mental faculties; a boy's business when he goes to school is to learn, that is, to store up things in his memory. For some years his intellect is little more than an instrument for taking in facts, or a receptacle for storing them; he welcomes them as fast as they come to him; he lives on what is without; he has his eyes ever about him; he has a lively 110 susceptibility of impressions; he imbibes information of every kind; and little does he make his own in a true sense of the word, living rather upon his neighbours all around him. He has opinions, religious, political, and literary, and, for a boy, is very positive in them and sure about them; but he gets them

1. Newman's Oxford University Sermons.

from his schoolfellows, or his masters, or his parents, as the case may be. Such as he is in his other relations, such also is he in his school exercises; his mind is observant, sharp, ready, retentive; he is almost passive in the acquisition of knowledge. I say this in no disparagement of the idea of a clever boy. Geography, chronology, history, language, natural history, he 120 heaps up the matter of these studies as treasures for a future day. It is the seven years of plenty with him: he gathers in by handfuls, like the Egyptians, without counting; and though, as time goes on, there is exercise for his argumentative powers in the Elements of Mathematics, and for his taste in the Poets and Orators, still, while at school, or at least, till quite the last years of his time, he acquires, and little more; and when he is leaving for the University, he is mainly the creature of foreign influences and circumstances, and made up of accidents, homogeneous or not, as the case may be. Moreover, the moral 130 habits, which are a boy's praise, encourage and assist this result; that is, diligence, assiduity, regularity, despatch, persevering application; for these are the direct conditions of acquisition, and naturally lead to it. Acquirements, again, are emphatically producible, and at a moment; they are a something to show, both for master and scholar; an audience, even though ignorant themselves of the subjects of an examination, can comprehend when questions are answered and when they are not. Here again is a reason why mental culture is in the minds of men identified with the acquisition of knowledge.   140

The same notion possesses the public mind, when it passes on from the thought of a school to that of a University: and with the best of reasons so far as this, that there is no true culture without requirements, and that philosophy presupposes knowledge. It requires a great deal of reading, or a wide range of information, to warrant us in putting forth our opinions on any serious subject; and without such learning the most original mind may be able indeed to dazzle, to amuse, to refute, to perplex, but not to come to any useful result or any trustworthy conclusion. There are indeed persons who   150

profess a different view of the matter, and even act upon it.
Every now and then you will find a person of vigorous or
fertile mind, who relies upon his own resources, despises all
former authors, and gives the world, with the utmost fear-
lessness, his views upon religion, or history, or any other popular subject. And his works may sell for a while; he may get a
name in his day; but this will be all. His readers are sure to
find on the long run that his doctrines are mere theories, and
not the expression of facts, that they are chaff instead of bread,
160 and then his popularity drops as suddenly as it rose.

Knowledge then is the indispensable condition of expansion
of mind, and the instrument of attaining to it; this cannot be
denied, it is ever to be insisted on; I begin with it as a first
principle; however, the very truth of it carries men too far,
and confirms to them the notion that it is the whole of the
matter. A narrow mind is thought to be that which contains
little·knowledge; and an enlarged mind, that which holds a
great deal; and what seems to put the matter beyond dispute
is, the fact of the great number of studies which are pursued
170 in a University, by its very profession. Lectures are given on
every kind of subject; examinations are held; prizes awarded.
There are moral, metaphysical, physical Professors; Professors
of languages, of history, of mathematics, of experimental science. Lists of questions are published, wonderful for their
range and depth, variety and difficulty; treatises are written,
which carry upon their very face the evidence of extensive
reading or multifarious information; what then is wanting for
mental culture to a person of large reading and scientific attainments? what is grasp of mind but acquirement? where
180 shall philosophical repose be found, but in the consciousness
and enjoyment of large intellectual possessions?

And yet this notion is, I conceive, a mistake, and my present
business is to show that it is one, and that the end of a Liberal
Education is not mere knowledge, or knowledge considered
in its *matter;* and I shall best attain my object, by actually
setting down some cases, which will be generally granted to

be instances of the process of enlightenment or enlargement
of mind, and others which are not, and thus, by the comparison, you will be able to judge for yourselves, Gentlemen,
whether Knowledge, that is, acquirement, is after all the real   190
principle of the enlargement, or whether that principle is not
rather something beyond it.

4

For instance,[2] let a person, whose experience has hitherto
been confined to the more calm and unpretending scenery of
these islands, whether here or in England, go for the first time
into parts where physical nature puts on her wilder and more
awful forms, whether at home or abroad, as into mountainous
districts; or let one, who has ever lived in a quiet village, go for
the first time to a great metropolis,—then I suppose he will
have a sensation which perhaps he never had before. He has a   200
feeling not in addition or increase of former feelings, but of
something different in its nature. He will perhaps be borne
forward, and find for a time that he has lost his bearings. He
has made a certain progress, and he has a consciousness of
mental enlargement; he does not stand where he did, he has a
new centre, and a range of thoughts to which he was before a
stranger.

Again, the view of the heavens which the telescope opens
upon us, if allowed to fill and possess the mind, may almost
whirl it round and make it dizzy. It brings in a flood of ideas,   210
and is rightly called an intellectual enlargement, whatever is
meant by the term.

And so again, the sight of beasts of prey and other foreign
animals, their strangeness, the originality (if I may use the
term) of their forms and gestures and habits and their variety
and independence of each other, throw us out of ourselves

2. The pages which follow are taken almost *verbatim* from the author's 14th (Oxford) University Sermon, which, at the time of writing
this Discourse, he did not expect ever to reprint.

into another creation, and as if under another Creator, if I may so express the temptation which may come on the mind. We seem to have new faculties, or a new exercise for our faculties, 220 by this addition to our knowledge; like a prisoner, who, having been accustomed to wear manacles or fetters, suddenly finds his arms and legs free.

Hence Physical Science generally, in all its departments, as bringing before us the exuberant riches and resources, yet the orderly course, of the Universe, elevates and excites the student, and at first, I may say, almost takes away his breath, while in time it exercises a tranquilizing influence upon him.

Again, the study of history is said to enlarge and enlighten the mind, and why? because, as I conceive, it gives it a power 230 of judging of passing events, and of all events, and a conscious superiority over them, which before it did not possess.

And in like manner, what is called seeing the world, entering into active life, going into society, travelling, gaining acquaintance with the various classes of the community, coming into contact with the principles and modes of thought of various parties, interests, and races, their views, aims, habits and manners, their religious creeds and forms of worship—gaining experience how various yet how alike men are, how lowminded, how bad, how opposed, yet how confident in their 240 opinions; all this exerts a perceptible influence upon the mind, which it is impossible to mistake, be it good or be it bad, and is popularly called its enlargement.

And then again, the first time the mind comes across the arguments and speculations of unbelievers, and feels what a novel light they cast upon what he has hitherto accounted sacred; and still more, if it gives in to them and embraces them, and throws off as so much prejudice what it has hitherto held, and, as if waking from a dream, begins to realize to its imagination that there is now no such thing as law and the 250 transgression of law, that sin is a phantom, and punishment a bugbear, that it is free to sin, free to enjoy the world and the flesh; and still further, when it does enjoy them, and reflects that it may think and hold just what it will, that "the world is all before it where to choose," [3] and what system to build up as its own private persuasion; when this torrent of wilful thoughts rushes over and inundates it, who will deny that the fruit of the tree of knowledge, or what the mind takes for knowledge, has made it one of the gods, with a sense of expansion and elevation,—an intoxication in reality, still, so far as the subjective state of the mind goes, an illumination? Hence 260 the fanaticism of individuals or nations, who suddenly cast off their Maker. Their eyes are opened; and, like the judgment-stricken king in the Tragedy,[4] they see two suns, and a magic universe, out of which they look back upon their former state of faith and innocence with a sort of contempt and indignation, as if they were then but fools, and the dupes of imposture.

On the other hand, Religion has its own enlargement, and an enlargement, not of tumult, but of peace. It is often remarked of uneducated persons, who have hitherto thought 270 little of the unseen world, that, on their turning to God, looking into themselves, regulating their hearts, reforming their conduct, and meditating on death and judgment, heaven and hell, they seem to become, in point of intellect, different beings from what they were. Before, they took things as they came, and thought no more of one thing than another. But now every event has a meaning; they have their own estimate of whatever happens to them; they are mindful of times and seasons, and compare the present with the past; and the world, no longer dull, monotonous, unprofitable, and hopeless, is a 280 various and complicated drama, with parts and an object, and an awful moral.

5

Now from these instances, to which many more might be added, it is plain, first, that the communication of knowledge

3. *Paradise Lost,* xii, 646.   4. Euripides, *Bacchae.*

certainly is either a condition or the means of that sense of enlargement or enlightenment, of which at this day we hear so
much in certain quarters: this cannot be denied; but next, it
is equally plain, that such communication is not the whole of
the process. The enlargement consists, not merely in the pas-
290 sive reception into the mind of a number of ideas hitherto unknown to it, but in the mind's energetic and simultaneous
action upon and towards and among those new ideas, which
are rushing in upon it. It is the action of a formative power,
reducing to order and meaning the matter of our acquirements; it is a making the objects of our knowledge subjectively
our own, or, to use a familiar word, it is a digestion of what
we receive, into the substance of our previous state of thought;
and without this no enlargement is said to follow. There is no
enlargement, unless there be a comparison of ideas one with
300 another, as they come before the mind, and a systematizing
of them. We feel our minds to be growing and expanding
then, when we not only learn, bur refer what we learn to what
we know already. It is not the mere addition to our knowledge
that is the illumination; but the locomotion, the movement on-
wards, of that mental centre, to which both what we know,
and what we are learning, the accumulating mass of our acquirements, gravitates. And therefore a truly great intellect,
and recognized to be such by the common opinion of mankind, such as the intellect of Aristotle, or of St. Thomas, or of
310 Newton, or of Goethe, (I purposely take instances within and
without the Catholic pale, when I would speak of the intellect
as such,) is one which takes a connected view of old and new,
past and present, far and near, and which has an insight into
the influence of all these one on another; without which there
is no whole, and no centre. It possesses the knowledge, not only
of things, but also of their mutual and true relations; knowledge, not merely considered as acquirement, but as philosophy.

Accordingly, when this analytical, distributive, harmonizing
process is away, the mind experiences no enlargement, and is
320 not reckoned as enlightened or comprehensive, whatever it

may add to its knowledge. For instance, a great memory,
have already said, does not make a philosopher, any more
than a dictionary can be called a grammar. There are men
who embrace in their minds a vast multitude of ideas, but with
little sensibility about their real relations towards each other.
These may be antiquarians, annalists, naturalists; they may be
learned in the law; they may be versed in statistics; they are
most useful in their own place; I should shrink from speaking
disrespectfully of them; still, there is nothing in such attainments to guarantee the absence of narrowness of mind. If they   330
are nothing more than well-read men, or men of information,
they have not what specially deserves the name of culture of
mind, or fulfils the type of Liberal Education.

In like manner, we sometimes fall in with persons who have
seen much of the world, and of the men who, in their day,
have played a conspicuous part in it, but who generalize nothing, and have no observation, in the true sense of the word.
They abound in information in detail, curious and entertaining, about men and things; and, having lived under the influence of no very clear or settled principles, religious or political,   340
they speak of every one and every thing, only as so many
phenomena, which are complete in themselves, and lead to
nothing, not discussing them, or teaching any truth, or in-
structing the hearer, but simply talking. No one would say
that these persons, well informed as they are, had attained to
any great culture of intellect or to philosophy.

The case is the same still more strikingly where the persons
in question are beyond dispute men of inferior powers and
deficient education. Perhaps they have been much in foreign
countries, and they receive, in a passive, otiose, unfruitful way,   350
the various facts which are forced upon them there. Seafaring
men, for example, range from one end of the earth to the
other; but the multiplicity of external objects, which they have
encountered, forms no symmetrical and consistent picture
upon their imagination; they see the tapestry of human life, as
it were on the wrong side, and it tells no story. They sleep, and

they rise up, and they find themselves, now in Europe, now in Asia; they see visions of great cities and wild regions; they are in the marts of commerce, or amid the islands of the South; 360 they gaze on Pompey's Pillar, or on the Andes; and nothing which meets them carries them forward or backward, to any idea beyond itself. Nothing has a drift or relation; nothing has a history or a promise. Every thing stands by itself, and comes and goes in its turn, like the shifting scenes of a show, which leave the spectator where he was. Perhaps you are near such a man on a particular occasion, and expect him to be shocked or perplexed at something which occurs; but one thing is much the same to him as another, or, if he is perplexed, it is as not knowing what to say, whether it is right to admire, or to 370 ridicule, or to disapprove, while conscious that some expression of opinion is expected from him; for in fact he has no standard of judgment at all, and no landmarks to guide him to a conclusion. Such is mere acquisition, and, I repeat, no one would dream of calling it philosophy.

6

Instances, such as these, confirm, by the contrast, the conclusion I have already drawn from those which preceded them. That only is true enlargement of mind which is the power of viewing many things at once as one whole, of referring them severally to their true place in the universal system, of under- 380 standing their respective values, and determining their mutual dependence. Thus is that form of Universal Knowledge, of which I have on a former occasion spoken, set up in the individual intellect, and constitutes its perfection. Possessed of this real illumination, the mind never views any part of the extended subject-matter of Knowledge without recollecting that it is but a part, or without the associations which spring from this recollection. It makes every thing in some sort lead to every thing else; it would communicate the image of the whole to every separate portion, till that whole becomes in imagination like a spirit, everywhere pervading and penetrating its 390 component parts, and giving them one definite meaning. Just as our bodily organs, when mentioned, recall their function in the body, as the word "creation" suggests the Creator, and "subjects" a sovereign, so, in the mind of the Philosopher, as we are abstractedly conceiving of him, the elements of the physical and moral world, sciences, arts, pursuits, ranks, offices, events, opinions, individualities, are all viewed as one, with correlative functions, and as gradually by successive combinations converging, one and all, to the true centre.

To have even a portion of this illuminative reason and true 400 philosophy is the highest state to which nature can aspire, in the way of intellect; it puts the mind above the influences of chance and necessity, above anxiety, suspense, unsettlement, and superstition, which is the lot of the many. Men, whose minds are possessed with some one object, take exaggerated views of its importance, are feverish in the pursuit of it, make it the measure of things which are utterly foreign to it, and are startled and despond if it happens to fail them. They are ever in alarm or in transport. Those on the other hand who have no object or principle whatever to hold by, lose their way, every 410 step they take. They are thrown out, and do not know what to think or say, at every fresh juncture; they have no view of persons, or occurrences, or facts, which come suddenly upon them, and they hang upon the opinion of others, for want of internal resources. But the intellect, which has been disciplined to the perfection of its powers, which knows, and thinks while it knows, which has learned to leaven the dense mass of facts and events with the elastic force of reason, such an intellect cannot be partial, cannot be exclusive, cannot be impetuous, cannot be at a loss, cannot but be patient, collected, and majes- 420 tically calm, because it discerns the end in every beginning, the origin in every end, the law in every interruption, the limit in each delay; because it ever knows where it stands, and how its path lies from one point to another. It is the τετράγωνος [5] of the Peripatetic, and has the "nil admirari" [6] of the Stoic,—

> *Felix qui potuit rerum cognoscere causas,*
> *Atque metus omnes, et inexorabile fatum*
> *Subjecit pedibus, strepitumque Acherontis avari.*[7]

There are men who, when in difficulties, originate at the moment vast ideas or dazzling projects; who, under the influence of excitement, are able to cast a light, almost as if from inspiration, on a subject or course of action which comes before them; who have a sudden presence of mind equal to any emergency, rising with the occasion, and an undaunted magnanimous bearing, and an energy and keenness which is but made intense by opposition. This is genius, this is heroism; it is the exhibition of a natural gift, which no culture can teach, at which no Institution can aim; here, on the contrary, we are concerned, not with mere nature, but with training and teaching. That perfection of the Intellect, which is the result of Education, and its *beau ideal,* to be imparted to individuals in their respective measures, is the clear, calm, accurate vision and comprehension of all things, as far as the finite mind can embrace them, each in its place, and with its own characteristics upon it. It is almost prophetic from its knowledge of history; it is almost heart-searching from its knowledge of human nature; it has almost supernatural charity from its freedom from littleness and prejudice; it has almost the repose of faith, because nothing can startle it; it has almost the beauty and harmony of heavenly contemplation, so intimate is it with the eternal order of things and the music of the spheres.

5. four-square man. Aristotle, *Nicomachean Ethics,* I, x, 11.   6. to wonder at nothing. Horace, *Epistles,* I, vi, i.   7. Happy is he who is able to know the sequence of things, and thus triumphs over all fear, and inexorable fate, and the roar of greedy Acheron. Vergil, *Georgics,* ii, 490-492.

7

And now, if I may take for granted that the true and adequate end of intellectual training and of a University is not Learning or Acquirement, but rather, is Thought or Reason exercised upon Knowledge, or what may be called Philosophy, I shall be in a position to explain the various mistakes which at the present day beset the subject of University Education.

I say then, if we would improve the intellect, first of all, we must ascend; we cannot gain real knowledge on a level; we must generalize, we must reduce to method, we must have a grasp of principles, and group and shape our acquisitions by means of them. It matters not whether our field of operation be wide or limited; in every case, to command it, is to mount above it. Who has not felt the irritation of mind and impatience created by a deep, rich country, visited for the first time, with winding lanes, and high hedges, and green steeps, and tangled woods, and every thing smiling indeed, but in a maze? The same feeling comes upon us in a strange city, when we have no map of its streets. Hence you hear of practised travellers, when they first come into a place, mounting some high hill or church tower, by way of reconnoitring its neighbourhood. In like manner, you must be above your knowledge, not under it, or it will oppress you; and the more you have of it, the greater will be the load. The learning of a Salmasius or a Burman, unless you are its master, will be your tyrant. "Imperat aut servit!" [8] if you can wield it with a strong arm, it is a great weapon; otherwise,

> *Vis consili expers*
> *Mole ruit suâ.*[9]

You will be overwhelmed, like Tarpeia, by the heavy wealth which you have exacted from tributary generations.

8. It either commands or serves. Horace, *Epistles,* I, x, 48.   9. Force without discretion falls of its own weight. Horace, *Odes,* III, iv, 65.

Instances abound; there are authors who are as pointless as they are inexhaustible in their literary resources. They measure knowledge by bulk, as it lies in the rude block, without symmetry, without design. How many commentators are there on the Classics, how many on Holy Scripture, from whom we rise up, wondering at the learning which has passed before us, and wondering why it passed! How many writers are there of Ecclesiastical History, such as Mosheim or Du Pin, who, 490 breaking up their subject into details, destroy its life, and defraud us of the whole by their anxiety about the parts! The Sermons, again, of the English Divines in the seventeenth century, how often are they mere repertories of miscellaneous and officious learning! Of course Catholics also may read without thinking; and in their case, equally as with Protestants, it holds good, that such knowledge is unworthy of the name, knowledge which they have not thought through, and thought out. Such readers are only possessed by their knowledge, not possessed of it; nay, in matter of fact they are often even car- 500 ried away by it, without any volition of their own. Recollect, the Memory can tyrannize, as well as the Imagination. Derangement, I believe, has been considered as a loss of control over the sequence of ideas. The mind, once set in motion, is henceforth deprived of the power of initiation, and becomes the victim of a train of associations, one thought suggesting another, in the way of cause and effect, as if by a mechanical process, or some physical necessity. No one, who has had experience of men of studious habits, but must recognize the existence of a parallel phenomenon in the case of those who 510 have over-stimulated the Memory. In such persons Reason acts almost as feebly and as impotently as in the madman; once fairly started on any subject whatever, they have no power of self-control; they passively endure the succession of impulses which are evolved out of the original exciting cause; they are passed on from one idea to another and go steadily forward, plodding along one line of thought in spite of the amplest concessions of the hearer, or wandering from it in endless digression in spite of his remonstrances. Now, if, as is very certain, no one would envy the madman the glow and originality of his conceptions, why must we extol the cultivation of that in-   520 tellect, which is the prey, not indeed of barren fancies but of barren facts, of random intrusions from without, though not of morbid imaginations from within? And in thus speaking, I am not denying that a strong and ready memory is in itself a real treasure; I am not disparaging a well-stored mind, though it be nothing besides, provided it be sober, any more than I would despise a bookseller's shop:—it is of great value to others, even when not so to the owner. Nor am I banishing, far from it, the possessors of deep and multifarious learning from my ideal University; they adorn it in the eyes of men; I do but   530 say that they constitute no type of the results at which it aims; that it is no great gain to the intellect to have enlarged the memory at the expense of faculties which are indisputably higher.

8

Nor indeed am I supposing that there is any great danger, at least in this day, of over-education; the danger is on the other side. I will tell you, Gentlemen, what has been the prac-tical error of the last twenty years,—not to load the memory of the student with a mass of undigested knowledge, but to force upon him so much that he has rejected all. It has been   540 the error of distracting and enfeebling the mind by an un-meaning profusion of subjects; of implying that a smattering in a dozen branches of study is not shallowness, which it really is, but enlargement, which it is not; of considering an ac-quaintance with the learned names of things and persons, and the possession of clever duodecimos, and attendance on elo-quent lecturers, and membership with scientific institutions, and the sight of the experiments on a platform and the speci-mens of a museum, that all this was not dissipation of mind, but progress. All things now are to be learned at once, not first   550 one thing, then another, not one well, but many badly. Learning is to be without exertion, without attention, without toil; without grounding, without advance, without finishing. There is to be nothing individual in it; and this, forsooth, is the wonder of the age. What the steam engine does with matter, the printing press is to do with mind; it is to act mechanically, and the population is to be passively, almost unconsciously enlightened, by the mere multiplication and dissemination of volumes. Whether it be the school boy, or the 560 school girl, or the youth at college, or the mechanic in the town, or the politician in the senate, all have been the victims in one way or other of this most preposterous and pernicious of delusions. Wise men have lifted up their voices in vain; and at length, lest their own institutions should be outshone and should disappear in the folly of the hour, they have been obliged, as far as they could with a good conscience, to humour a spirit which they could not withstand, and make temporizing concessions at which they could not but inwardly smile.

It must not be supposed that, because I so speak, therefore I 570 have some sort of fear of the education of the people: on the contrary, the more education they have, the better, so that it is really education. Nor am I an enemy to the cheap publication of scientific and literary works, which is now in vogue: on the contrary, I consider it a great advantage, convenience, and gain; that is, to those to whom education has given a capacity for using them. Further, I consider such innocent recreations as science and literature are able to furnish will be a very fit occupation of the thoughts and the leisure of young persons, and may be made the means of keeping them from bad 580 employments and bad companions. Moreover, as to that superficial acquaintance with chemistry, and geology, and astronomy, and political economy, and modern history, and biography, and other branches of knowledge, which periodical literature and occasional lectures and scientific institutions diffuse through the community, I think it a graceful accomplishment, and a suitable, nay, in this day a necessary accomplishment, in the case of educated men. Nor, lastly, am I disparaging or discouraging the thorough acquisition of any one of these studies, or denying that, as far as it goes, such thorough acquisition is a real education of the mind. All I say is, call things by their right names, and do not confuse together ideas which are essentially different. A thorough knowledge of one science and a superficial acquaintance with many, are not the same thing; a smattering of a hundred things or a memory for detail, is not a philosophical or comprehensive view. Recreations are not education; accomplishments are not education. Do not say, the people must be educated, when, after all, you only mean, amused, refreshed, soothed, put into good spirits and good humour, or kept from vicious excesses. I do not say that such amusements, such occupations of mind, are not a great gain; but they are not education. You may as well call drawing and fencing education, as a general knowledge of botany or conchology. Stuffing birds or playing stringed instruments is an elegant pastime, and a resource to the idle, but it is not education; it does not form or cultivate the intellect. Education is a high word; it is the preparation for knowledge, and it is the imparting of knowledge in proportion to that preparation. We require intellectual eyes to know withal, as bodily eyes for sight. We need both objects and organs intellectual; we cannot gain them without setting about it; we cannot gain them in our sleep, or by hap-hazard. The best telescope does not dispense with eyes; the printing press or the lecture room will assist us greatly, but we must be true to ourselves, we must be parties in the work. A University is, according to the usual designation, an Alma Mater, knowing her children one by one, not a foundry, or a mint, or a treadmill.

9

I protest to you, Gentlemen, that if I had to choose between a so-called University, which dispensed with residence and tutorial superintendence, and gave its degrees to any person who passed an examination in a wide range of subjects, and a

University which had no professors or examinations at all, but merely brought a number of young men together for three or four years and then sent them away as the University of Oxford is said to have done some sixty years since, if I were asked which of these two methods was the better discipline of the intellect,—mind, I do not say which is *morally* the better, for it is plain that compulsory study must be a good and idleness an intolerable mischief,—but if I must determine which of the
630 two courses was the more successful in training, moulding, enlarging the mind, which sent out men the more fitted for their secular duties, which produced better public men, men of the world, men whose names would descend to posterity, I have no hesitation in giving the preference to that University which did nothing, over that which exacted of its members an acquaintance with every science under the sun. And, paradox as this may seem, still if results be the test of systems, the influence of the public schools and colleges of England, in the course of the last century, at least will bear out one side of the
640 contrast as I have drawn it. What would come, on the other hand, of the ideal systems of education which have fascinated the imagination of this age, could they ever take effect, and whether they would not produce a generation frivolous, narrow-minded, and resourceless, intellectually considered, is a fair subject for debate; but so far is certain, that the Universities and scholastic establishments, to which I refer, and which did little more than bring together first boys and then youths in large numbers, these institutions, with miserable deformities on the side of morals, with a hollow profession of
650 Christianity, and a heathen code of ethics,—I say, at least they can boast of a succession of heroes and statesmen, of literary men and philosophers, of men conspicuous for great natural virtues, for habits of business, for knowledge of life, for practical judgment, for cultivated tastes, for accomplishments, who have made England what it is,—able to subdue the earth, able to domineer over Catholics.

How is this to be explained? I suppose as follows: When a

multitude of young men, keen, open-hearted, sympathetic, and observant, as young men are, come together and freely mix with each other, they are sure to learn one from another, 660 even if there be no one to teach them; the conversation of all is a series of lectures to each, and they gain for themselves new ideas and views, fresh matter of thought, and distinct principles for judging and acting, day by day. An infant has to learn the meaning of the information which its senses convey to it, and this seems to be its employment. It fancies all that the eye presents to it to be close to it, till it actually learns the contrary, and thus by practice does it ascertain the relations and uses of those first elements of knowledge which are necessary for its animal existence. A parallel teaching is necessary 670 for our social being, and it is secured by a large school or a college; and this effect may be fairly called in its own department an enlargement of mind. It is seeing the world on a small field with little trouble; for the pupils or students come from very different places, and with widely different notions, and there is much to generalize, much to adjust, much to eliminate, there are inter-relations to be defined, and conventional rules to be established, in the process, by which the whole assemblage is moulded together, and gains one tone and one character. 680

Let it be clearly understood, I repeat it, that I am not taking into account moral or religious considerations; I am but saying that that youthful community will constitute a whole, it will embody a specific idea, it will represent a doctrine, it will administer a code of conduct, and it will furnish principles of thought and action. It will give birth to a living teaching, which in course of time will take the shape of a self-perpetuating tradition, or a *genius loci,* as it is sometimes called; which haunts the home where it has been born, and which imbues and forms, more or less, and one by one, every indi- 690 vidual who is successively brought under its shadow. Thus it is that, independent of direct instruction on the part of Superiors, there is a sort of self-education in the academic institutions of Protestant England; a characteristic tone of thought, a recognized standard of judgment is found in them, which, as developed in the individual who is submitted to it, becomes a twofold source of strength to him, both from the distinct stamp it impresses on his mind, and from the bond of union which it creates between him and others,—effects which are 700 shared by the authorities of the place, for they themselves have been educated in it, and at all times are exposed to the influence of its ethical atmosphere. Here then is a real teaching, whatever be its standards and principles, true or false; and it at least tends towards cultivation of the intellect; it at least recognizes that knowledge is something more than a sort of passive reception of scraps and details; it is a something, and it does a something, which never will issue from the most strenuous efforts of a set of teachers, with no mutual sympathies and no inter-communion, of a set of examiners with no opinions 710 which they dare profess, and with no common principles, who are teaching or questioning a set of youths who do not know them, and do not know each other, on a large number of subjects, different in kind, and connected by no wide philosophy, three times a week, or three times a year, or once in three years, in chill lecture-rooms or on a pompous anniversary.

10

Nay, self-education in any shape, in the most restricted sense, is preferable to a system of teaching which, professing so much, really does so little for the mind. Shut your College gates against the votary of knowledge, throw him back upon 720 the searchings and the efforts of his own mind; he will gain by being spared an entrance into your Babel. Few indeed there are who can dispense with the stimulus and support of instructors, or will do any thing at all, if left to themselves. And fewer still (though such great minds are to be found), who will not, from such unassisted attempts, contract a self-reliance and a self-esteem, which are not only moral evils, but serious hindrances to the attainment of truth. And next to none, perhaps, or none, who will not be reminded from time to time of the disadvantage under which they lie, by their imperfect ground- ing, by the breaks, deficiencies, and irregularities of their 730 knowledge, by the eccentricity of opinion and the confusion of principle which they exhibit. They will be too often ignorant of what every one knows and takes for granted, of that multi- tude of small truths which fall upon the mind like dust, impal- pable and ever accumulating; they may be unable to converse, they may argue perversely, they may pride themselves on their worst paradoxes or their grossest truisms, they may be full of their own mode of viewing things, unwilling to be put out of their way, slow to enter into the minds of others;—but, with these and whatever other liabilities upon their heads, they are 740 likely to have more thought, more mind, more philosophy, more true enlargement, than those earnest but ill-used persons, who are forced to load their minds with a score of subjects against an examination, who have too much on their hands to indulge themselves in thinking or investigation, who devour premiss and conclusion together with indiscriminate greedi- ness, who hold whole sciences on faith, and commit demon- strations to memory, and who too often, as might be expected, when their period of education is passed, throw up all they have learned in disgust, having gained nothing really by their 750 anxious labours, except perhaps the habit of application.

Yet such is the better specimen of the fruit of that ambitious system which has of late years been making way among us: for its result on ordinary minds, and on the common run of students, is less satisfactory still; they leave their place of edu- cation simply dissipated and relaxed by the multiplicity of sub- jects, which they have never really mastered, and so shallow as not even to know their shallowness. How much better, I say, is it for the active and thoughtful intellect, where such is to be found, to eschew the College and the University alto- 760 gether, than to submit to a drudgery so ignoble, a mockery so contumelious! How much more profitable for the independent mind, after the mere rudiments of education, to range through a library at random, taking down books as they meet him, and pursuing the trains of thought which his mother wit suggests! How much healthier to wander into the fields, and there with the exiled Prince to find "tongues in the trees, books in the running brooks!" [9] How much more genuine an education is that of the poor boy in the Poem [10]—a Poem, whether in 770 conception or in execution, one of the most touching in our language—who, not in the wide world, but ranging day by day around his widowed mother's home, "a dexterous gleaner" in a narrow field, and with only such slender outfit

> as the village schools and books a few
> Supplied,

contrived from the beach, and the quay, and the fisher's boat, and the inn's fireside, and the tradesman's shop, and the shepherd's walk, and the smuggler's hut, and the mossy moor, and the screaming gulls, and the restless waves, to fashion for 780 himself a philosophy and a poetry of his own!

But in a large subject, I am exceeding my necessary limits. Gentlemen, I must conclude abruptly; and postpone any summing up of my argument, should that be necessary, to another day.

---

9. Shakespeare, *As You Like It,* Act II, Scene 1.   10. Crabbe's "Tales of the Hall." This Poem, let me say, I read on its first publication, above thirty years ago, with extreme delight, and have never lost my love of it; and on taking it up lately, found I was even more touched by it than heretofore. A work which can please in youth and age, seems to fulfil (in logical language) the *accidental definition* of a Classic.

III

KNOWLEDGE VIEWED IN RELATION
TO PROFESSIONAL SKILL

I

I have been insisting, in my two preceding Discourses, first, on the cultivation of the intellect, as an end which may reasonably be pursued for its own sake; and next, on the nature of that cultivation, or what that cultivation consists in. Truth of whatever kind is the proper object of the intellect; its cultivation then lies in fitting it to apprehend and contemplate truth. Now the intellect in its present state, with exceptions which need not here be specified, does not discern truth intuitively, or as a whole. We know, not by a direct and simple vision, not at a glance, but, as it were, by piecemeal and accumulation, by a mental process, by going round an object, by the comparison, the combination, the mutual correction, the continual adaptation, of many partial notions, by the employment, concentration, and joint action of many faculties and exercises of mind. Such a union and concert of the intellectual powers, such an enlargement and development, such a comprehensiveness, is necessarily a matter of training. And again, such a training is a matter of rule; it is not mere application, however exemplary, which introduces the mind to truth, nor the reading many books, nor the getting up many subjects, nor the witnessing many experiments, nor the attending many lectures. All this is short of enough; a man may have done it all, yet be lingering in the vestibule of knowledge:— he may not realize what his mouth utters; he may not see with his mental eye what confronts him; he may have no grasp of things as they are; or at least he may have no power at all of advancing one step forward of himself, in consequence of

what he has already acquired, no power of discriminating
between truth and falsehood, of sifting out the grains of truth
30 from the mass, of arranging things according to their real
value, and, if I may use the phrase, of building up ideas. Such
a power is the result of a scientific formation of mind; it is an
acquired faculty of judgment, of clearsightedness, of sagacity,
of wisdom, of philosophical reach of mind, and of intellectual
self-possession and repose,—qualities which do not come of
mere acquirement. The bodily eye, the organ for apprehend-
ing material objects, is provided by nature; the eye of the
mind, of which the object is truth, is the work of discipline
and habit.

40 This process of training, by which the intellect, instead of
being formed or sacrificed to some particular or accidental
purpose, some specific trade or profession, or study or science,
is disciplined for its own sake, for the perception of its own
proper object, and for its own highest culture, is called Liberal
Education; and though there is no one in whom it is carried
as far as is conceivable, or whose intellect would be a pattern
of what intellects should be made, yet there is scarcely any
one but may gain an idea of what real training is, and at least
look towards it, and make its true scope and result, not some-
50 thing else, his standard of excellence; and numbers there are
who may submit themselves to it, and secure it to themselves
in good measure. And to set forth the right standard, and to
train according to it, and to help forward all students toward
it according to their various capacities, this I conceive to be
the business of a University.

2

Now this is what some great men are very slow to allow;
they insist that Education should be confined to some particular and narrow end, and should issue in some definite work,
which can be weighed and measured. They argue as if every
60 thing, as well as every person, had its price; and that where

there has been a great outlay, they have a right to expect a re-
turn in kind. This they call making Education and Instruction
"useful," and "Utility" becomes their watchword. With a fun-
damental principle of this nature, they very naturally go on to
ask, what there is to show for the expense of a University;
what is the real worth in the market of the article called "a
Liberal Education," on the supposition that it does not teach us
definitely how to advance our manufactures, or to improve our
lands, or to better our civil economy; or again, if it does not at
once make this man a lawyer, that an engineer, and that a   70
surgeon; or at least if it does not lead to discoveries in chemistry, astronomy, geology, magnetism, and science of every kind.

This question, as might have been expected, has been keenly
debated in the present age, and formed one main subject of
the controversy, to which I referred in the Introduction to the
present Discourses, as having been sustained in the first decade
of this century by a celebrated Northern Review [1] on the one
hand, and defenders of the University of Oxford on the other.
Hardly had the authorities of that ancient seat of learning,
waking from their long neglect, set on foot a plan for the edu-   80
cation of the youth committed to them, than the representatives of science and literature in the city, which has sometimes
been called the Northern Athens,[2] remonstrated, with their
gravest arguments and their most brilliant satire, against the
direction and shape which the reform was taking. Nothing
would content them, but that the University should be set to
rights on the basis of the philosophy of Utility; a philosophy,
as they seem to have thought, which needed but to be pro-
claimed in order to be embraced. In truth, they were little
aware of the depth and force of the principles on which the   90
academical authorities were proceeding, and, this being so, it
was not to be expected that they would be allowed to walk
at leisure over the field of controversy which they had selected.
Accordingly they were encountered in behalf of the Univer-

1. *The Edinburgh Review.*   2. Edinburgh.

sity by two men of great name and influence in their day, of
very different minds, but united, as by Collegiate ties, so in the
clear-sighted and large view which they took of the whole
subject of Liberal Education; and the defence thus provided
for the Oxford studies has kept its ground to this day.

3

100   Let me be allowed to devote a few words to the memory
of distinguished persons, under the shadow of whose name I
once lived, and by whose doctrine I am now profiting. In the
heart of Oxford there is a small plot of ground hemmed in by
public thoroughfares, which has been the possession and the
home of one Society for above five hundred years. In the old
time of Boniface the Eighth and John the Twenty-second, in
the age of Scotus and Occam and Dante, before Wiclif or Huss
had kindled those miserable fires which are still raging to the
ruin of the highest interests of man, an unfortunate king of
110   England, Edward the Second, flying from the field of Ban-
nockburn, is said to have made a vow to the Blessed Virgin to
found a religious house in her honour, if he got back in safety.
Prompted and aided by his Almoner, he decided on placing
this house in the city of Alfred; and the Image of Our Lady,
which is opposite its entrance-gate, is to this day the token of
the vow and its fulfilment. King and Almoner have long been
in the dust, and strangers have entered into their inheritance,
and their creed has been forgotten, and their holy rites dis-
owned; but day by day a memento is still made in the holy
120   Sacrifice by at least one Catholic Priest, once a member of that
College, for the souls of those Catholic benefactors who fed
him there for so many years. The visitor, whose curiosity has
been excited by its present fame, gazes perhaps with something of disappointment on a collection of buildings which
have with them so few of the circumstances of dignity or
wealth. Broad quadrangles, high halls and chambers, orna-
mented cloisters, stately walks, or umbrageous gardens, a

throng of students, ample revenues, or a glorious history, none
of these things were the portion of that old Catholic foundation; nothing in short which to the common eye sixty years   130
ago would have given tokens of what it was to be. But it had
at that time a spirit working within it, which enabled its in-
mates to do, amid its seeming insignificance, what no other
body in the place could equal; not a very abstruse gift or
extraordinary boast, but a rare one, the honest purpose to administer the trust committed to them in such a way as their
conscience pointed out as best. So, whereas the Colleges of
Oxford are self-electing bodies, the fellows in each perpetually
filling up for themselves the vacancies which occur in their
number, the members of this foundation determined, at a time   140
when, either from evil custom or from ancient statute, such a
thing was not known elsewhere, to throw open their fellow-
ships to the competition of all comers, and, in the choice of
associates henceforth, to cast to the winds every personal motive and feeling, family connexion, and friendship, and patron-
age, and political interest, and local claim, and prejudice, and
party jealousy, and to elect solely on public and patriotic
grounds. Nay, with a remarkable independence of mind, they
resolved that even the table of honours, awarded to literary
merit by the University in its new system of examination for   150
degrees, should not fetter their judgment as electors; but that
at all risks, and whatever criticism it might cause, and whatever odium they might incur, they would select the men, who-
ever they were, to be children of their Founder, whom they
thought in their consciences to be most likely from their intellectual and moral qualities to please him, if (as they expressed
it) he were still upon earth, most likely to do honour to his
College, most likely to promote the objects which they believed
he had at heart. Such persons did not promise to be the disciples of a low Utilitarianism; and consequently, as their   160
collegiate reform synchronized with that reform of the Academical body, in which they bore a principal part, it was not
unnatural that, when the storm broke upon the University

from the North, their Alma Mater, whom they loved, should have found her first defenders within the walls of that small College, which had first put itself into a condition to be her champion.

These defenders, I have said, were two, of whom the more distinguished was the late Dr. Copleston, then a Fellow of the
170 College, successively its Provost, and Protestant Bishop of Llandaff. In that Society, which owes so much to him, his name lives, and ever will live, for the distinction which his talents bestowed on it, for the academical importance to which he raised it, for the generosity of spirit, the liberality of sentiment, and the kindness of heart, with which he adorned it, and which even those who had least sympathy with some aspects of his mind and character could not but admire and love. Men come to their meridian at various periods of their lives; the last years of the eminent person I am speaking of
180 were given to duties which, I am told, have been the means of endearing him to numbers, but which afforded no scope for that peculiar vigour and keenness of mind which enabled him, when a young man, single-handed, with easy gallantry, to encounter and overthrow the charge of three giants of the North combined against him. I believe I am right in saying that, in the progress of the controversy, the most scientific, the most critical, and the most witty, of that literary company, all of them now, as he himself, removed from this visible scene, Professor Playfair, Lord Jeffrey, and the Rev. Sydney Smith,
190 threw together their several efforts into one article of their Review, in order to crush and pound to dust the audacious controvertist who had come out against them in defence of his own Institutions. To have even contended with such men was a sufficient voucher for his ability, even before we open his pamphlets, and have actual evidence of the good sense, the spirit, the scholar-like taste, and the purity of style, by which they are distinguished.

He was supported in the controversy, on the same general principles, but with more of method and distinctness, and, I

will add, with greater force and beauty and perfection, both 200
of thought and of language, by the other distinguished writer,
to whom I have already referred, Mr. Davison; who, though
not so well known to the world in his day, has left more behind
him than the Provost of Oriel, to make his name remembered
by posterity. This thoughtful man, who was the admired and
intimate friend of a very remarkable person, whom, whether
he wish it or not, numbers revere and love as the first author
of the subsequent movement in the Protestant Church towards
Catholicism,[3] this grave and philosophical writer, whose
works I can never look into without sighing that such a man 210
was lost to the Catholic Church, as Dr. Butler[4] before him,
by some early bias or some fault of self-education—he, in a
review of a work by Mr. Edgeworth on Professional Education, which attracted a good deal of attention in its day, goes
leisurely over the same ground, which had already been
rapidly traversed by Dr. Copleston, and, though professedly
employed upon Mr. Edgeworth, is really replying to the
northern critic who had brought that writer's work into notice,
and to a far greater author than either of them, who in a past
age had argued on the same side. 220

4

The author to whom I allude is no other than Locke.[5] That
celebrated philosopher has preceded the Edinburgh Reviewers
in condemning the ordinary subjects in which boys are instructed at school, on the ground that they are not needed by
them in after life; and before quoting what his disciples have
said in the present century, I will refer to a few passages of
the master. " 'Tis matter of astonishment," he says in his work
on Education, "that men of quality and parts should suffer

3. Mr. Keble, Vicar of Hursley, late Fellow of Oriel, and Professor of
Poetry in the University of Oxford. 4. Joseph Butler, English bishop,
author of *Analogy of Religion*. 5. John Locke, author of *Essay Con-
cerning the Human Understanding*.

themselves to be so far misled by custom and implicit faith.
Reason, if consulted with, would advise, that their children's
time should be spent in acquiring what might be *useful* to
them, when they come to be men, rather than that their heads
should be stuffed with a deal of trash, a great part whereof
they usually never do ('tis certain they never need to) think
on again as long as they live; and so much of it as does stick by
them they are only the worse for."

And so again, speaking of verse-making, he says, "I know
not what reason a father can have to wish his son a poet, who
does not desire him to *bid defiance to all other callings and
business;* which is not yet the worst of the case; for, if he
proves a successful rhymer, and gets once the reputation of a
wit, I desire it to be considered, what company and places he
is likely to spend his time in, nay, and estate too; for it is very
seldom seen that any one discovers *mines of gold or silver in
Parnassus.* 'Tis a pleasant air, but a barren soil."

In another passage he distinctly limits utility in education
to its bearing on the future profession or trade of the pupil,
that is, he scorns the idea of any education of the intellect,
simply as such. "Can there be any thing more ridiculous," he
asks, "than that a father should waste his own money, and his
son's time, in setting him to *learn the Roman language,* when
at the same time he *designs him for a trade,* wherein he, having no use of Latin, fails not to forget that little which he
brought from school, and which 'tis ten to one he abhors for
the ill-usage it procured him? Could it be believed, unless we
have every where amongst us examples of it, that a child
should be forced to learn the rudiments of a language, which
he is never to use in the course of life that he is designed to,
and neglect all the while the writing a good hand, and casting
accounts, which are of great advantage in all conditions of
life, and to most trades indispensably necessary?" [6] Nothing
of course can be more absurd than to neglect in education

6. Locke, *Of Education,* Sections 94, 174, 164.

those matters which are necessary for a boy's future calling; but the tone of Locke's remarks evidently implies more than this, and is condemnatory of any teaching which tends to the general cultivation of the mind.

Now to turn to his modern disciples. The study of the Classics had been made the basis of the Oxford education, in the reforms which I have spoken of, and the Edinburgh Reviewers protested, after the manner of Locke, that no good   270 could come of a system which was not based upon the principle of Utility.

"Classical Literature," they said, "is the great object at Oxford. Many minds, so employed, have produced many works and much fame in that department; but if all liberal arts and sciences, *useful to human life,* had been taught there, if *some* had dedicated themselves to *chemistry, some to mathematics, some* to *experimental philosophy,* and if *every* attainment had been honoured in the mixt ratio of its difficulty and *utility,* the system of such a University would have been much more valu-   280 able, but the splendour of its name something less."

Utility may be made the end of education, in two respects: either as regards the individual educated, or the community at large. In which light do these writers regard it? in the latter. So far they differ from Locke, for they consider the advancement of science as the supreme and real end of a University. This is brought into view in the sentences which follow.

"When a University has been doing *useless* things for a long time, it appears at first degrading to them to be *useful.* A set of Lectures on Political Economy would be discouraged in   290 Oxford, probably despised, probably not permitted. To discuss the inclosure of commons, and to dwell upon imports and exports, to come so near to common life, would seem to be undignified and contemptible. In the same manner, the Parr or the Bentley [7] of the day would be scandalized, in a University, to be put on a level with the discoverer of a neutral salt;

7. Classical scholars.

and yet, *what other measure is there of dignity in intellectual labour but usefulness?* And what ought the term University to mean, but a place where every science is taught which is 300 liberal, and at the same time useful to mankind? Nothing would so much tend to bring classical literature within proper bounds as *a steady and invariable appeal to utility* in our appreciation of all human knowledge. . . . *Looking always to real utility as our guide,* we should see, with equal pleasure, a studious and inquisitive mind arranging the productions of nature, investigating the qualities of bodies, or mastering the difficulties of the learned languages. We should not care whether he was chemist, naturalist, or scholar, because we know it to be as *necessary* that matter should be studied and 310 subdued *to the use of man,* as that taste should be gratified, and imagination inflamed."

Such then is the enunciation, as far as words go, of the theory of Utility in Education; and both on its own account, and for the sake of the able men who have advocated it, it has a claim on the attention of those whose principles I am here representing. Certainly it is specious to contend that nothing is worth pursuing but what is useful; and that life is not long enough to expend upon interesting, or curious, or brilliant trifles. Nay, in one sense, I will grant it is more than specious, 320 it is true; but, if so, how do I propose directly to meet the objection? Why, Gentlemen, I have really met it already, viz., in laying down, that intellectual culture is its own end; for what has its *end* in itself, has its *use* in itself also. I say, if a Liberal Education consists in the culture of the intellect, and if that culture be in itself a good, here, without going further, is an answer to Locke's question; for if a helathy body is a good in itself, why is not a healthy intellect? and if a College of Physicians is a useful institution, because it contemplates bodily health, why is not an Academical Body, though it were 330 simply and solely engaged in imparting vigour and beauty and grasp to the intellectual portion of our nature? And the Reviewers I am quoting seem to allow this in their better moments, in a passage which, putting aside the question of its justice in fact, is sound and true in the principles to which it appeals:—

"The present state of classical education," they say, "cultivates the *imagination* a great deal too much, and other *habits of mind* a great deal too little, and trains up many young men in a style of elegant imbecility, utterly unworthy of the talents with which nature has endowed them. . . . The 340 matter of fact is, that a classical scholar of twenty-three or twenty-four is a man principally conversant with works of imagination. His feelings are quick, his fancy lively, and his taste good. Talents for *speculation* and *original inquiry* he has none, nor has he formed the invaluable *habit of pushing things up to their first principles,* or of collecting dry and unamusing facts as the materials for reasoning. All the solid and masculine parts of his *understanding* are left wholly without cultivation; he hates the pain of thinking, and suspects every man whose boldness and originality call upon him 350 to defend his opinions and prove his assertions."

5

Now, I am not at present concerned with the specific question of classical education; else, I might reasonably question the justice of calling an intellectual discipline, which embraces the study of Aristotle, Thucydides, and Tacitus, which involves Scholarship and Antiquities, *imaginative;* still so far I readily grant, that the cultivation of the "understanding," of a "talent for speculation and original inquiry," and of "the habit of pushing things up to their first principles," is a principal portion of a *good* or *liberal* education. If then the Reviewers 360 consider such cultivation the characteristic of a *useful* education, as they seem to do in the foregoing passage, it follows, that what they mean by "useful" is just what I mean by "good" or "liberal:" and Locke's question becomes a verbal one. Whether youths are to be taught Latin or verse-making will depend on the *fact,* whether these studies tend to mental culture; but, however this is determined, so far is clear, that in that mental culture consists what I have called a liberal or non-professional, and what the Reviewers call a useful education.

370   This is the obvious answer which may be made to those who urge upon us the claims of Utility in our plans of Education; but I am not going to leave the subject here: I mean to take a wider view of it. Let us take "useful," as Locke takes it, in its proper and popular sense, and then we enter upon a large field of thought, to which I cannot do justice in one Discourse, though to-day's is all the space that I can give to it. I say, let us take "useful" to mean, not what is simply good, but what *tends* to good, or is the *instrument* of good; and in this sense also, Gentlemen, I will show you how a liberal education is

380 truly and fully a useful, though it be not a professional, education. "Good" indeed means one thing, and "useful" means another; but I lay it down as a principle, which will save us a great deal of anxiety, that, though the useful is not always good, the good is always useful. Good is not only good, but reproductive of good; this is one of its attributes; nothing is excellent, beautiful, perfect, desirable for its own sake, but it overflows, and spreads the likeness of itself all around it. Good is prolific; it is not only good to the eye, but to the taste; it not only attracts us, but it communicates itself; it excites first our

390 admiration and love, then our desire and our gratitude, and that, in proportion to its intenseness and fulness in particular instances. A great good will impart great good. If then the intellect is so excellent a portion of us, and its cultivation so excellent, it is not only beautiful, perfect, admirable, and noble in itself, but in a true and high sense it must be useful to the possessor and to all around him; not useful in any low, mechanical, mercantile sense, but as diffusing good, or as a blessing, or a gift, or power, or a treasure, first to the owner, then through him to the world. I say then, if a liberal education be

400 good, it must necessarily be useful too.

6

You will see what I mean by the parallel of bodily health. Health is a good in itself, though nothing came of it, and is especially worth seeking and cherishing; yet, after all, the blessings which attend its presence are so great, while they are so close to it and so redound back upon it and encircle it, that we never think of it except as useful as well as good, and praise and prize it for what it does, as well as for what it is, though at the same time we cannot point out any definite and distinct work or production which it can be said to effect. And so as regards intellectual culture, I am far from denying utility in this large sense as the end of Education, when I lay it down, that the culture of the intellect is a good in itself and its own end; I do not exclude from the idea of intellectual culture what it cannot but be, from the very nature of things; I only deny that we must be able to point out, before we have any right to call it useful, some art, or business, or profession, or trade, or work, as resulting from it, and as its real and complete end. The parallel is exact:—As the body may be sacrificed to some manual or other toil, whether moderate or oppressive, so may the intellect be devoted to some specific profession; and I do not call *this* the culture of the intellect. Again, as some member or organ of the body may be inordinately used and developed, so may memory, or imagination, or the reasoning faculty; and *this* again is not intellectual culture. On the other hand, as the body may be tended, cherished, and exercised with a simple view to its general health, so may the intellect also be generally exercised in order to its perfect state; and this *is* its cultivation.

Again, as health ought to precede labour of the body, and as a man in health can do what an unhealthy man cannot do, and as of this health the properties are strength, energy, agility, graceful carriage and action, manual dexterity, and endurance of fatigue, so in like manner general culture of mind is the best aid to professional and scientific study, and educated men can

do what illiterate cannot; and the man who has learned to
think and to reason and to compare and to discriminate and to
analyze, who has refined his taste, and formed his judgment,
and sharpened his mental vision, will not indeed at once be a
lawyer, or a pleader, or an orator, or a statesman, or a physi-
440 cian, or a good landlord, or a man of business, or a soldier, or
an engineer, or a chemist, or a geologist, or an antiquarian, but
he will be placed in that state of intellect in which he can take
up any one of the sciences or callings I have referred to, or any
other for which he has a taste or special talent, with an ease, a
grace, a versatility, and a success, to which another is a
stranger. In this sense then, and as yet I have said but a very
few words on a large subject, mental culture is emphatically
useful.

If then I am arguing, and shall argue, against Professional
450 or Scientific knowledge as the sufficient end of a University
Education, let me not be supposed, Gentlemen, to be disre-
spectful towards particular studies, or arts, or vocations, and
those who are engaged in them. In saying that Law or Medicine is not the end of a University course, I do not mean to
imply that the University does not teach Law or Medicine.
What indeed can it teach at all, if it does not teach something
particular? It teaches *all* knowledge by teaching all *branches*
of knowledge, and in no other way. I do but say that there
will be this distinction as regards a Professor or Law, or of
460 Medicine, or of Geology, or of Political Economy, in a University and out of it, that out of a University he is in danger of
being absorbed and narrowed by his pursuit, and of giving
Lectures which are the Lectures of nothing more than a
lawyer, physician, geologist, or political economist; whereas in
a University he will just know where he and his science stand,
he has come to it, as it were, from a height, he has taken a
survey of all knowledge, he is kept from extravagance by the
very rivalry of other studies, he has gained from them a special
illumination and largeness of mind and freedom and self-
470 possession, and he treats his own in consequence with a

philosophy and a resource, which belongs not to the study itself, but to his liberal education.

This then is how I should solve the fallacy, for so I must call it, by which Locke and his disciples would frighten us from cultivating the intellect, under the notion that no education is useful which does not teach us some temporal calling, or some mechanical art, or some physical secret, I say that a cultivated intellect, because it is a good in itself, brings with it a power and a grace to every work and occupation which it undertakes, and enables us to be more useful, and to a greater   480 number. There is a duty we owe to human society as such, to the state to which we belong, to the sphere in which we move, to the individuals towards whom we are variously related, and whom we successively encounter in life; and that philosophical or liberal education, as I have called it, which is the proper function of a University, if it refuses the foremost place to professional interests, does but postpone them to the formation of the citizen, and, while it subserves the larger interests of philanthropy, prepares also for the successful prosecution of those merely personal objects, which at first sight it seems   490 to disparage.

7

And now, Gentlemen, I wish to be allowed to enforce in detail what I have been saying, by some extracts from the writings to which I have already alluded, and to which I am so greaty indebted.

"It is an undisputed maxim in Political Economy," says Dr. Copleston, "that the separation of professions and the division of labour tend to the perfection of every art, to the wealth of nations, to the general comfort and well-being of the community. This principle of division is in some instances pur-   500 sued so far as to excite the wonder of people to whose notice it is for the first time pointed out. There is no saying to what extent it may not be carried; and the more the powers of each individual are concentrated in one employment, the greater

skill and quickness will he naturally display in performing it.
But, while he thus contributes more effectually to the accumulation of national wealth, he becomes himself more and more
degraded as a rational being. In proportion as his sphere of
action is narrowed his mental powers and habits become con-
510 tracted; and he resembles a subordinate part of some powerful
machinery, useful in its place, but insignificant and worthless
out of it. If it be necessary, as it is beyond all question necessary, that society should be split into divisions and subdivisions, in order that its several duties may be well performed,
yet we must be careful not to yield up ourselves wholly and
exclusively to the guidance of this system; we must observe
what its evils are, and we should modify and restrain it, by
bringing into action other principles, which may serve as a
check and counterpoise to the main force.

520 "There can be no doubt that every art is improved by con-
fining the professor of it to that single study. But, *although
the art itself is advanced by this concentration of mind in its
service, the individual who is confined to it goes back*. The
advantage of the community is nearly in an inverse ratio with
his own.

"Society itself requires some other contribution from each
individual, besides the particular duties of his profession. And,
if no such liberal intercourse be established, it is the common
failing of human nature, to be engrossed with petty views
530 and interests, to underrate the importance of all in which we
are not concerned, and to carry our partial notions into cases
where they are inapplicable, to act, in short, as so many un-
connected units, displacing and repelling one another.

"In the cultivation of literature is found that common link,
which, among the higher and middling departments of life,
unites the jarring sects and subdivisions into one interest,
which supplies common topics, and kindles common feelings, unmixed with those narrow prejudices with which all
professions are more or less infected. The knowledge, too,
540 which is thus acquired, expands and enlarges the mind, excites

its faculties, and calls those limbs and muscles into freer exercise which, by too constant use in one direction, not only acquire an illiberal air, but are apt also to lose somewhat of their native play and energy. And thus, without directly qualifying a man for any of the employments of life, it enriches and ennobles all. Without teaching him the peculiar business of any one office or calling, it enables him to act his part in each of them with better grace and more elevated carriage; and, if happily planned and conducted, is a main ingredient in that complete and generous education which fits a man 'to per- 550 form justly, skilfully, and magnanimously, all the offices, both private and public, of peace and war.' " 8

8

The view of liberal education, advocated in these extracts, is expanded by Mr. Davison in the Essay to which I have already referred. He lays more stress on the "usefulness" of Liberal Education in the larger sense of the word than his predecessor in the controversy. Instead of arguing that the Utility of knowledge to the individual varies inversely with its Utility to the public, he chiefly employs himself on the sug- gestions contained in Dr. Copleston's last sentences. He shows, 560 first, that a Liberal Education is something far higher, even in the scale of Utility, than what is commonly called a Use- ful Education, and next, that it is necessary or useful for the purposes even of that Professional Education which com- only engrosses the title of Useful. The former of these two theses he recommends to us in an argument from which the following passages are selected:—

"It is to take a very contracted view of life," he says, "to think with great anxiety how persons may be educated to superior skill in their department, comparatively neglecting 570 or excluding the more liberal and enlarged cultivation. In his

8. John Milton, "Of Education."

(Mr. Edgeworth's) system, the value of every attainment is to be measured by its subserviency to a calling. The specific duties of that calling are exalted at the cost of those free and independent tastes and virtues which come in to sustain the common relations of society, and raise the individual in them. In short, a man is to be usurped by his profession. He is to be clothed in its garb from head to foot. His virtues, his science, and his ideas are all to be put into a gown or uniform, and the 580 whole man to be shaped, pressed, and stiffened, in the exact mould of his technical character. Any interloping accomplishments, or a faculty which cannot be taken into public pay, if they are to be indulged in him at all, must creep along under the cloak of his more serviceable privileged merits. Such is the state of perfection to which the spirit and general tendency of this system would lead us.

"But the professional character is not the only one which a person engaged in a profession has to support. He is not always upon duty. There are services he owes, which are neither 590 parochial, nor forensic, nor military, nor to be described by any such epithet of civil regulation, and yet are in no wise inferior to those that bear these authoritative titles; inferior neither in their intrinsic value, nor their moral import, nor their impression upon society. As a friend, as a companion, as a citizen at large; in the connections of domestic life; in the improvement and embellishment of his leisure, he has a sphere of action, revolving, if you please, within the sphere of his profession, but not clashing with it; in which if he can show none of the advantages of an improved understanding, what-600 ever may be his skill or proficiency in the other, he is no more than an ill-educated man.

"There is a certain faculty in which all nations of any refinement are great practitioners. It is not taught at school or college as a distinct science; though it deserves that what is taught there should be made to have some reference to it; nor is it endowed at all by the public; everybody being obliged to exercise it for himself in person, which he does to the best of his skill. But in nothing is there a greater difference than in the manner of doing it. The advocates of professional learning will smile when we tell them that this same faculty which we would have encouraged, is simply that of speaking good sense in English, without fee or reward, in common conversation. They will smile when we lay some stress upon it; but in reality it is no such trifle as they imagine. Look into the huts of savages, and see, for there is nothing to listen to, the dismal blank of their stupid hours of silence; their professional avocations of war and hunting are over; and, having nothing to do, they have nothing to say. Turn to improved life, and you find conversation in all its forms the medium of something more than an idle pleasure; indeed, a very active agent in circulating and forming the opinions, tastes, and feelings of a whole people. It makes of itself a considerable affair. Its topics are the most promiscuous—all those which do not belong to any particular province. As for its power and influence, we may fairly say that it is of just the same consequence to a man's immediate society, how he talks, as how he acts. Now of all those who furnish their share to rational conversation, a mere adept in his own art is universally admitted to be the worst. The sterility and uninstructiveness of such a person's social hours are quite proverbial. Or if he escape being dull, it is only by launching into ill-timed, learned loquacity. We do not desire of him lectures or speeches; and he has nothing else to give. Among benches he may be powerful; but seated on a chair he is quite another person. On the other hand, we may affirm, that one of the best companions is a man who, to the accuracy and research of a profession, has joined a free excursive acquaintance with various learning, and caught from it the spirit of general observation."

9

Having thus shown that a liberal education is a real benefit to the subjects of it, as members of society, in the various duties and circumstances and accidents of life, he goes on, in the next place, to show that, over and above those direct services which might fairly be expected of it, it actually subserves the discharge of those particular functions, and the pursuit of those particular advantages, which are connected with professional exertion, and to which Professional Education is directed.

"We admit," he observes, "that when a person makes a business of one pursuit, he is in the right way to eminence in it; 650 and that divided attention will rarely give excellence in many. But our assent will go no further. For, to think that the way to prepare a person for excelling in any one pursuit (and that is the only point in hand), is to fetter his early studies, and cramp the first development of his mind, by a reference to the exigencies of that pursuit barely, is a very different notion, and one which, we apprehend, deserves to be exploded rather than received. Possibly a few of the abstract, insulated kinds of learning might be approached in that way. The exceptions to be made are very few, and need not be recited. But for the 660 acquisition of professional and practical ability such maxims are death to it. The main ingredients of that ability are requisite knowledge and cultivated faculties; but, of the two, the latter is by far the chief. A man of well improved faculties has the command of another's knowledge. A man without them, has not the command of his own.

"Of the intellectual powers, the judgment is that which takes the foremost lead in life. How to form it to the two habits it ought to possess, of exactness and vigour, is the problem. It would be ignorant presumption so much as to hint at any 670 routine of method by which these qualities may with certainty be imparted to every or any understanding. Still, however, we may safely lay it down that they are not to be got 'by a gatherer of simples,' but are the combined essence and extracts of many different things, drawn from much varied reading and discipline, first, and observation afterwards. For if there be a single intelligible point on this head, it is that a man who has been trained to think upon one subject or for one subject only, will never be a good judge even in that one: whereas the enlargement of his circle gives him increased knowledge and power in a rapidly increasing ratio. So much do ideas act, not 680 as solitary units, but by grouping and combination; and so clearly do all the things that fall within the proper province of the same faculty of the mind, intertwine with and support each other. Judgment lives as it were by comparison and discrimination. Can it be doubted, then, whether the range and extent of that assemblage of things upon which it is practised in its first essays are of use to its power?

"To open our way a little further on this matter, we will define what we mean by the power of judgment; and then try to ascertain among what kind of studies the improvement of 690 it may be expected at all.

"Judgment does not stand here for a certain homely, useful quality of intellect, that guards a person from committing mistakes to the injury of his fortunes or common reputation; but for that master-principle of business, literature, and talent, which gives him strength in any subject he chooses to grapple with, and enables him to *seize the strong point* in it. Whether this definition be metaphysically correct or not, it comes home to the substance of our inquiry. It describes the power that every one desires to possess when he comes to act in a profes- 700 sion, or elsewhere; and corresponds with our best idea of a cultivated mind.

"Next, it will not be denied, that in order to do any good to the judgment, the mind must be employed upon such subjects as come within the cognizance of that faculty, and give some real exercise to its perceptions. Here we have a rule of selection by which the different parts of learning may be classed for our purpose. Those which belong to the province of the judgment are religion (in its evidences and interpretation), ethics, history, eloquence, poetry, theories of general 710 speculation, the fine arts, and works of wit. Great as the variety of these large divisions of learning may appear, they are all held in union by two capital principles of connexion. First, they are all quarried out of one and the same great subject of man's moral, social, and feeling nature. And secondly, they are all under the control (more or less strict) of the same power of moral reason."

"If these studies," he continues, "be such as give a direct play and exercise to the faculty of the judgment, then they are
720 the true basis of education for the active and inventive powers, whether destined for a profession or any other use. Miscellaneous as the assemblage may appear, of history, eloquence, poetry, ethics, etc., blended together, they will all conspire in an union of effect. They are necessary mutually to explain and interpret each other. The knowledge derived from them all will amalgamate, and the habits of a mind versed and practised in them by turns will join to produce a richer vein of thought and of more general and practical application than could be obtained of any single one, as the fusion of the metals
730 into Corinthian brass gave the artist his most ductile and perfect material. Might we venture to imitate an author (whom indeed it is much safer to take as an authority than to attempt to copy), Lord Bacon, in some of his concise illustrations of the comparative utility of the different studies,[9] we should say that history would give fulness, moral philosophy strength, and poetry elevation to the understanding. Such in reality is the natural force and tendency of the studies; but there are few minds susceptible enough to derive from them any sort of virtue adequate to those high expressions. We must be con-
740 tented therefore to lower our panegyric to this, that a person cannot avoid receiving some infusion and tincture, at least, of those several qualities, from that course of diversified reading. One thing is unquestionable, that the elements of general reason are not to be found fully and truly expressed in any one kind of study; and that he who would wish to know her idiom, must read it in many books.

9. Bacon, "Of Studies."

"If different studies are useful for aiding, they are still more useful for correcting each other; for as they have their particular merits severally, so they have their defects, and the most extensive acquaintance with one can produce only an 750 intellect either too flashy or too jejune, or infected with some other fault of confined reading. History, for example, shows things as they are, that is, the morals and interests of men disfigured and perverted by all their imperfections of passion, folly, and ambition; philosophy strips the picture too much; poetry adorns it too much; the concentrated lights of the three correct the false peculiar colouring of each, and show us the truth. The right mode of thinking upon it is to be had from them taken all together, as every one must know who has seen their united contributions of thought and feeling expressed in 760 the masculine sentiment of our immortal statesman, Mr. Burke, whose eloquence is inferior only to his more admirable wisdom. If any mind improved like his, is to be our instructor, we must go to the fountain head of things as he did, and study not his works but his method; by the one we may become feeble imitators, by the other arrive at some ability of our own. But, as all biography assures us, he, and every other able thinker, has been formed, not by a parsimonious admeasurement of studies to some definite future object (which is Mr. Edgeworth's maxim), but by taking a wide and liberal com- 770 pass, and thinking a great deal on many subjects with no better end in view than because the exercise was one which made them more rational and intelligent beings."

10

But I must bring these extracts to an end. To-day I have confined myself to saying that that training of the intellect, which is best for the individual himself, best enables him to discharge his duties to society. The Philosopher, indeed, and the man of the world differ in their very notion, but the methods, by which they are respectively formed, are pretty

780 much the same. The Philosopher has the same command of
matters of thought, which the true citizen and gentleman has
of matters of business and conduct. If then a practical end
must be assigned to a University course, I say it is that of
training good members of society. Its art is the art of social
life, and its end is fitness for the world. It neither confines its
views to particular professions on the one hand, nor creates
heroes or inspires genius on the other. Works indeed of genius
fall under no art; heroic minds come under no rule; a University is not a birthplace of poets or of immortal authors, of
790 founders of schools, leaders of colonies, or conquerors of
nations. It does not promise a generation of Aristotles or New-
tons, of Napoleons or Washingtons, of Raphaels or Shake-
speares, though such miracles of nature it has before now
contained within its precincts. Nor is it content on the other
hand with forming the critic or the experimentalist, the economist or the engineer, though such too it includes within its
scope. But a University training is the great ordinary means
to a great but ordinary end; it aims at raising the intellectual
tone of society, at cultivating the public mind, at purifying
800 the national taste, at supplying true principles to popular
enthusiasm and fixed aims to popular aspiration, at giving
enlargement and sobriety to the ideas of the age, at facilitating
the exercise of political power, and refining the intercourse of
private life. It is the education which gives a man a clear
conscious view of his own opinions and judgments, a truth in
developing them, an eloquence in expressing them, and a
force in urging them. It teaches him to see things as they are,
to go right to the point, to disentangle a skein of thought, to
detect what is sophistical, and to discard what is irrelevant.
810 It prepares him to fill any post with credit, and to master any
subject with facility. It shows him how to accommodate himself to others, how to throw himself into their state of mind,
how to bring before them his own, how to influence them,
how to come to an understanding with them, how to bear
with them. He is at home in any society, he has common

ground with every class; he knows when to speak and when to be silent; he is able to converse, he is able to listen; he can ask a question pertinently, and gain a lesson seasonably, when he has nothing to impart himself; he is ever ready, yet never in the way; he is a pleasant companion, and a comrade you can 820 depend upon; he knows when to be serious and when to trifle, and he has a sure tact which enables him to trifle with gracefulness and to be serious with effect. He has the repose of a mind which lives in itself, while it lives in the world, and which has resources for its happiness at home when it cannot go abroad. He has a gift which serves him in public, and supports him in retirement, without which good fortune is but vulgar, and with which failure and disappointment have a charm. The art which tends to make a man all this, is in the object which it pursues as useful as the art of wealth or the 830 art of health, though it is less susceptible of method, and less tangible, less certain, less complete in its result.

IV

KNOWLEDGE VIEWED IN RELATION
TO RELIGION

I

We shall be brought, Gentlemen, to-day, to the termination of the investigation which I commenced three Discourses back, and which, I was well aware, from its length, if for no other reason, would make demands upon the patience even of indulgent hearers.

First I employed myself in establishing the principle that Knowledge is its own reward; and I showed that, when considered in this light, it is called Liberal Knowledge, and is the scope of Academical Institutions.

10   Next, I examined what is meant by Knowledge, when it is said to be pursued for its own sake; and I showed that, in order satisfactorily to fulfil this idea, Philosophy must be its *form;* or, in other words, that its matter must not be admitted into the mind passively, as so much acquirement, but must be mastered and appropriated as a system consisting of parts, related one to the other, and interpretative of one another in the unity of a whole.

Further, I showed that such a philosophical contemplation of the field of Knowledge as a whole, leading, as it did, to an
20   understanding of its separate departments, and an appreciation of them respectively, might in consequence be rightly called an illumination; also, it was rightly called an enlargement of mind, because it was a distinct location of things one with another, as if in space; while it was moreover its proper cultivation and its best condition, both because it secured to the intellect the sight of things as they are, or of truth, in opposition to fancy, opinion, and theory; and again, because it presupposed and involved the perfection of its various powers.

Such, I said, was that Knowledge, which deserves to be
30   sought for its own sake, even though it promised no ulterior advantage. But, when I had got as far as this, I went farther, and observed that, from the nature of the case, what was so good in itself could not but have a number of external uses, though it did not promise them, simply because it *was* good; and that it was necessarily the source of benefits to society, great and diversified in proportion to its own intrinsic excellence. Just as in morals, honesty is the best policy, as being profitable in a secular aspect, though such profit is not the measure of its worth, so too as regards what may be called
40   the virtues of the Intellect, their very possession indeed is a substantial good, and is enough, yet still that substance has a shadow, inseparable from it, viz., its social and political usefulness. And this was the subject to which I devoted the preceding Discourse.

One portion of the subject remains:—this intellectual cul·

ture, which is so exalted in itself, not only has a bearing upon social and active duties, but upon Religion also. The educated mind may be said to be in a certain sense religious; that is, it has what may be considered a religion of its own, independent of Catholicism, partly cooperating with it, partly thwarting it; at once a defence yet a disturbance to the Church in Catholic countries,—and in countries beyond her pale, at one time in open warfare with her, at another in defensive alliance. The history of Schools and Academies, and of Literature and Science generally, will, I think, justify me in thus speaking. Since, then, my aim in these Discourses is to ascertain the function and the action of a University, viewed in itself, and its relations to the various instruments of teaching and training which are round about it, my survey of it would not be complete unless I attempted, as I now propose to do, to exhibit its general bearings upon Religion.

2

Right reason, that is, Reason rightly exercised, leads the mind to the Catholic Faith, and plants it there, and teaches it in all its religious speculations to act under its guidance. But Reason, considered as a real agent in the world, and as an operative principle in man's nature, with an historical course and with definite results, is far from taking so straight and satisfactory a direction. It considers itself from first to last independent and supreme; it requires no external authority; it makes a religion for itself. Even though it accepts Catholicism, it does not go to sleep; it has an action and development of its own, as the passions have, or the moral sentiments, or the principle of self-interest. Divine grace, to use the language of Theology, does not by its presence supersede nature; nor is nature at once brought into simple concurrence and coalition with grace. Nature pursues its course, now coincident with that of grace, now parallel to it, now across, now divergent, now counter, in proportion to its own imperfection and to the

attraction and influence which grace exerts over it. And what
takes place as regards other principles of our nature and their
developments is found also as regards the Reason. There is, we
know, a Religion of enthusiasm, of superstitious ignorance, of
statecraft; and each has that in it which resembles Catholicism, and that again which contradicts Catholicism. There is
the Religion of a warlike people, and of a pastoral people;
there is a Religion of rude times, and in like manner there is a
Religion of civilized times, of the cultivated intellect, of the
philosopher, scholar, and gentleman. This is that Religion of
Reason, of which I speak. Viewed in itself, however near it
comes to Catholicism, it is of course simply distinct from it;
for Catholicism is one whole, and admits of no compromise or
modification. Yet this is to view it in the abstract; in matter of
fact, and in reference to individuals, we can have no difficulty
in conceiving this philosophical Religion present in a Catholic
country, as a spirit influencing men to a certain extent, for
good or for bad or for both,—a spirit of the age, which again
may be found, as among Catholics, so with still greater sway
and success in a country not Catholic, yet specifically the same
in such a country as it exists in a Catholic community. The
problem then before us to-day, is to set down some portions of
the outline, if we can ascertain them, of the Religion of Civilization, and to determine how they lie relatively to those principles, doctrines, and rules, which Heaven has given us in the
Catholic Church.

And here again, when I speak of Revealed Truth, it is
scarcely necessary to say that I am not referring to the main
articles and prominent points of faith, as contained in the
Creed. Had I undertaken to delineate a philosophy, which
directly interfered with the Creed, I could not have spoken
of it as compatible with the profession of Catholicism. The
philosophy I speak of, whether it be viewed within or outside
the Church, does not necessarily take cognizance of the Creed.
Where the country is Catholic, the educated mind takes its
articles for granted, by a sort of implicit faith; where it is not,

it simply ignores them and the whole subject-matter to which they relate, as not affecting social and political interests. Truths about God's Nature, about His dealings towards the human race, about the Economy of Redemption,—in the one case it humbly accepts them, and passes on; in the other it passes them over, as matters of simple opinion, which never 120 can be decided, and which can have no power over us to make us morally better or worse. I am not speaking then of belief in the great objects of faith, when I speak of Catholicism, but I am contemplating Catholicism chiefly as a system of pastoral instruction and moral duty; and I have to do with its doctrines mainly as they are subservient to its direction of the conscience and the conduct. I speak of it, for instance, as teaching the ruined state of man; his utter inability to gain Heaven by any thing he can do himself; the moral certainty of his losing his soul if left to himself; the simple absence of all rights and 130 claims on the part of the creature in the presence of the Creator; the illimitable claims of the Creator on the service of the creature; the imperative and obligatory force of the voice of conscience; and the inconceivable evil of sensuality. I speak of it as teaching, that no one gains Heaven except by the free grace of God, or without a regeneration of nature; that no one can please Him without faith; that the heart is the seat both of sin and of obedience; that charity is the fulfilling of the Law; and that incorporation into the Catholic Church is the ordinary instrument of salvation. These are the lessons which dis- 140 tinguish Catholicism as a popular religion, and these are the subjects to which the cultivated intellect will practically be turned:—I have to compare and contrast, not the doctrinal, but the moral and social teaching of Philosophy on the one hand, and Catholicism on the other.

3

Now, on opening the subject, we see at once a momentous benefit which the philosopher is likely to confer on the pastors

of the Church. It is obvious that the first step which they have
to effect in the conversion of man and the renovation of his
150 nature, is his rescue from that fearful subjection to sense which
is his ordinary state. To be able to break through the meshes
of that thraldom, and to disentangle and to disengage its ten
thousand holds upon the heart, is to bring it, I might almost
say, half way to Heaven. Here, even divine grace, to speak of
things according to their appearances, is ordinarily baffled,
and retires, without expedient or resource, before this giant
fascination. Religion seems too high and unearthly to be able
to exert a continued influence upon us: its effort to rouse the
soul, and the soul's effort to co-operate, are too violent to last.
160 It is like holding out the arm at full length, or supporting
some great weight, which we manage to do for a time, but
soon are exhausted and succumb. Nothing can act beyond its
own nature; when then we are called to what is supernatural,
though those extraordinary aids from Heaven are given us,
with which obedience becomes possible, yet even with them
it is of transcendent difficulty. We are drawn down to earth
every moment with the ease and certainty of a natural gravita-
tion, and it is only by sudden impulses and, as it were, forcible
plunges that we attempt to mount upwards. Religion indeed
170 enlightens, terrifies, subdues; it gives faith, it inflicts remorse,
it inspires resolutions, it draws tears, it inflames devotion, but
only for the occasion. I repeat, it imparts an inward power
which ought to effect more than this; I am not forgetting
either the real sufficiency of its aids, nor the responsibility of
those in whom they fail. I am not discussing theological questions at all, I am looking at phenomena as they lie before me,
and I say that, in matter of fact, the sinful spirit repents, and
protests it will never sin again, and for a while is protected by
disgust and abhorrence from the malice of its foe. But that
180 foe knows too well that such seasons of repentance are wont
to have their end: he patiently waits, till nature faints with the
effort of resistance, and lies passive and hopeless under the
next access of temptation. What we need then is some expedi-

ent or instrument, which at least will obstruct and stave off
the approach of our spiritual enemy, and which is sufficiently
congenial and level with our nature to maintain as firm a hold
upon us as the inducements of sensual gratification. It will be
our wisdom to employ nature against itself. Thus sorrow,
sickness, and care are providential antagonists to our inward
disorders; they come upon us as years pass on, and generally   190
produce their natural effects on us, in proportion as we are
subjected to their influence. These, however, are God's instruments, not ours; we need a similar remedy, which we can
make our own, the object of some legitimate faculty, or the
aim of some natural affection, which is capable of resting on
the mind, and taking up its familiar lodging with it, and en-
grossing it, and which thus becomes a match for the besetting
power of sensuality, and a sort of homœopathic medicine for
the disease. Here then I think is the important aid which
intellectual cultivation furnishes to us in rescuing the victims   200
of passion and self-will. It does not supply religious motives; it
is not the cause or proper antecedent of any thing supernatural; it is not meritorious of heavenly aid or reward; but it
does a work, at least *materially* good (as theologians speak),
whatever be its real and formal character. It expels the excite-
ments of sense by its introduction of those of the intellect.

This then is the *primâ facie* advantage of the pursuit of
Knowledge; it is the drawing the mind off from things which
will harm it to subjects which are worthy a rational being;
and, though it does not raise it above nature, nor has any tend-   210
ency to make us pleasing to our Maker, yet is it nothing to
substitute what is in itself harmless for what is, to say the least,
inexpressibly dangerous? is it a little thing to exchange a circle
of ideas which are certainly sinful, for others which are certainly not so? You will say, perhaps, in the words of the
Apostle, "Knowledge puffeth up:" and doubtless this mental
cultivation, even when it is successful for the purpose for
which I am applying it, may be from the first nothing more
than the substitution of pride for sensuality. I grant it, I think

220 I shall have something to say on this point presently; but this is not a necessary result, it is but an incidental evil, a danger which may be realized or may be averted, whereas we may in most cases predicate guilt, and guilt of a heinous kind, where the mind is suffered to run wild and indulge its thoughts without training or law of any kind; and surely to turn away a soul from mortal sin is a good and a gain so far, whatever comes of it. And therefore, if a friend in need is twice a friend, I conceive that intellectual employments, though they do no more than occupy the mind with objects naturally noble or 230 innocent, have a special claim upon our consideration and gratitude.

4

Nor is this all: Knowledge, the discipline by which it is gained, and the tastes which it forms, have a natural tendency to refine the mind, and to give it an indisposition, simply natural, yet real, nay, more than this, a disgust and abhorrence, towards excesses and enormities of evil, which are often or ordinarily reached at length by those who are not careful from the first to set themselves against what is vicious and criminal. It generates within the mind a fastidiousness, analo- 240 gous to the delicacy or daintiness which good nurture or a sickly habit induces in respect of food; and this fastidiousness, though arguing no high principle, though no protection in the case of violent temptation, nor sure in its operation, yet will often or generally be lively enough to create an absolute loathing of certain offences, or a detestation and scorn of them as ungentlemanlike, to which ruder natures, nay, such as have far more of real religion in them, are tempted, or even betrayed. Scarcely can we exaggerate the value, in its place, of a safeguard such as this, as regards those multitudes who are 250 thrown upon the open field of the world, or are withdrawn from its eye and from the restraint of public opinion. In many cases, where it exists, sins, familiar to those who are otherwise circumstanced, will not even occur to the mind: in others, the

sense of shame and the quickened apprehension of detection
will act as a sufficient obstacle to them, when they do present
themselves before it. Then, again, the fastidiousness I am
speaking of will create a simple hatred of that miserable tone of
conversation which, obtaining as it does in the world, is a constant fuel of evil, heaped up round about the soul: moreover, it
will create an irresolution and indecision in doing wrong,   260
which will act as a *remora* [1] till the danger is past away. And
though it has no tendency, I repeat, to mend the heart, or to
secure it from the dominion in other shapes of those very evils
which it repels in the particular modes of approach by which
they prevail over others, yet cases may occur when it gives
birth, after sins have been committed, to so keen a remorse and
so intense a self-hatred, as are even sufficient to cure the particular moral disorder, and to prevent its accesses ever afterwards;—as the spendthrift in the story, who, after gazing on
his lost acres from the summit of an eminence, came down a   270
miser, and remained a miser to the end of his days.

And all this holds good in a special way, in an age such as
ours, when, although pain of body and mind may be rife as
heretofore, yet other counteractions of evil, of a penal character, which are present at other times, are away. In rude and
semi-barbarous periods, at least in a climate such as our own,
it is the daily, nay, the principal business of the senses, to convey feelings of discomfort to the mind, as far as they convey
feelings at all. Exposure to the elements, social disorder and
lawlessness, the tyranny of the powerful, and the inroads of   280
enemies, are a stern discipline, allowing brief intervals, or
awarding a sharp penance, to sloth and sensuality. The rude
food, the scanty clothing, the violent exercise, the vagrant life,
the military constraint, the imperfect pharmacy, which now
are the trials of only particular classes of the community, were
once the lot more or less of all. In the deep woods or the wild
solitudes of the medieval era, feelings of religion or supersti-

1. Hindrance, or delay.

tion were naturally present to the population, which in various
ways co-operated with the missionary or pastor, in retaining it
290 in a noble simplicity of manners. But, when in the advancement of society men congregate in towns, and multiply in
contracted spaces, and law gives them security, and art gives
them comforts, and good government robs them of courage
and manliness, and monotony of life throws them back upon
themselves, who does not see that diversion or protection from
evil they have none, that vice is the mere reaction of unhealthy
toil, and sensual excess the holyday of resourceless ignorance?
This is so well understood by the practical benevolence of the
day, that it has especially busied itself in plans for supplying
300 the masses of our town population with intellectual and honourable recreations. Cheap literature, libraries of useful and
entertaining knowledge, scientific lectureships, museums,
zoological collections, buildings and gardens to please the eye
and to give repose to the feelings, external objects of whatever
kind, which may take the mind off itself, and expand and
elevate it in liberal contemplations, these are the human means,
wisely suggested, and good as far as they go, for at least parry-
ing the assaults of moral evil, and keeping at bay the enemies,
not only of the individual soul, but of society at large.
310 Such are the instruments by which an age of advanced
civilization combats those moral disorders, which Reason as
well as Revelation denounces; and I have not been backward
to express my sense of their serviceableness to Religion. Moreover, they are but the foremost of a series of influences, which
intellectual culture exerts upon our moral nature, and all upon
the type of Christianity, manifesting themselves in veracity,
probity, equity, fairness, gentleness, benevolence, and ami-
ableness; so much so, that a character more noble to look at,
more beautiful, more winning, in the various relations of life
320 and in personal duties, is hardly conceivable, than may, or
might be, its result, when that culture is bestowed upon a soil
naturally adapted to virtue. If you would obtain a picture for
contemplation which may seem to fulfil the ideal, which the

Apostle has delineated under the name of charity, in its sweetness and harmony, its generosity, its courtesy to others, and its depreciation of self, you could not have recourse to a better furnished *studio* than to that of Philosophy, with the specimens of it, which with greater or less exactness are scattered through society in a civilized age. It is enough to refer you, Gentlemen, to the various Biographies and Remains of con- 330 temporaries and others, which from time to time issue from the press, to see how striking is the action of our intellectual upon our moral nature, where the moral material is rich, and the intellectual cast is perfect. Individuals will occur to all of us, who deservedly attract our love and admiration, and whom the world almost worships as the work of its own hands. Religious principle, indeed,—that is, faith,—is, to all appearance, simply away; the work is as certainly not supernatural as it is certainly noble and beautiful. This must be insisted on, that the Intellect may have its due; but it also must be insisted on 340 for the sake of conclusions to which I wish to conduct our investigation. The radical difference indeed of this mental refinement from genuine religion, in spite of its seeming relationship, is the very cardinal point on which my present discussion turns; yet, on the other hand, such refinement may readily be assigned to a Christian origin by hasty or distant observers, or by those who view it in a particular light. And as this is the case, I think it advisable, before proceeding with the delineation of its characteristic features, to point out to you distinctly the elementary principles on which its morality is based.   350

5

You will bear in mind then, Gentlemen, that I spoke just now of the scorn and hatred which a cultivated mind feels for some kinds of vice, and the utter disgust and profound humiliation which may come over it, if it should happen in any degree to be betrayed into them. Now this feeling may have its root in faith and love, but it may not; there is nothing really religious in it, considered by itself. Conscience indeed is implanted in the breast by nature, but it inflicts upon us fear as well as shame; when the mind is simply angry with itself and nothing more, surely the true import of the voice of nature and the depth of its intimations have been forgotten, and a false philosophy has misinterpreted emotions which ought to lead to God. Fear implies the transgression of a law, and a law implies a lawgiver and judge; but the tendency of intellectual culture is to swallow up the fear in the self-reproach, and self-reproach is directed and limited to our mere sense of what is fitting and becoming. Fear carries us out of ourselves, whereas shame may act upon us only within the round of our own thoughts. Such, I say, is the danger which awaits a civilized age; such is its besetting sin (not inevitable, God forbid! or we must abandon the use of God's own gifts), but still the ordinary sin of the Intellect; conscience tends to become what is called a moral sense; the command of duty is a sort of taste; sin is not an offence against God, but against human nature.

The less amiable specimens of this spurious religion are those which we meet not unfrequently in my own country. I can use with all my heart the poet's words,

> England, with all thy faults, I love thee still; [2]

but to those faults no Catholic can be blind. We find there men possessed of many virtues, but proud, bashful, fastidious, and reserved. Why is this? it is because they think and act as if there were really nothing objective in their religion; it is because conscience to them is not the word of a lawgiver, as it ought to be, but the dictate of their own minds and nothing more; it is because they do not look out of themselves, because they do not look through and beyond their own minds to their Maker, but are engrossed in notions of what is due to themselves, to their own dignity and their own consistency. Their conscience has become a mere self-respect. Instead of doing

2. Byron, "Beppo."

one thing and then another, as each is called for, in faith and 390
obedience, careless of what may be called the *keeping* of deed
with deed, and leaving Him who gives the command to blend
the portions of their conduct into a whole, their one object,
however unconscious to themselves, is to paint a smooth and
perfect surface, and to be able to say to themselves that they
have done their duty. When they do wrong, they feel, not
contrition, of which God is the object, but remorse, and a
sense of degradation. They call themselves fools, not sinners;
they are angry and impatient, not humble. They shut themselves up in themselves; it is misery to them to think or to 400
speak of their own feelings; it is misery to suppose that others
see them, and their shyness and sensitiveness often become
morbid. As to confession, which is so natural to the Catholic,
to them it is impossible; unless indeed, in cases where they
have been guilty, an apology is due to their own character, is
expected of them, and will be satisfactory to look back upon.
They are victims of an intense self-contemplation.

There are, however, far more pleasing and interesting forms
of this moral malady than that which I have been depicting:
I have spoken of the effect of intellectual culture on proud 410
natures; but it will show to greater advantage, yet with as
little approximation to religious faith, in amiable and un-
affected minds. Observe, Gentlemen, the heresy, as it may be
called, of which I speak, is the substitution of a moral sense
or taste for conscience in the true meaning of the word; now
this error may be the foundation of a character of far more
elasticity and grace than ever adorned the persons whom I
have been describing. It is especially congenial to men of an
imaginative and poetical cast of mind, who will readily accept
the notion that virtue is nothing more than the graceful in 420
conduct. Such persons, far from tolerating fear, as a principle,
in their apprehension of religious and moral truth, will not be
slow to call it simply gloom and superstition. Rather a philosopher's, a gentleman's religion, is of a liberal and generous
character; it is based upon honour; vice is evil, because it is

unworthy, despicable, and odious. This was the quarrel of the ancient heathen with Christianity, that, instead of simply fixing the mind on the fair and the pleasant, it intermingled other ideas with them of a sad and painful nature; that it
430 spoke of tears before joy, a cross before a crown; that it laid the foundation of heroism in penance; that it made the soul tremble with the news of Purgatory and Hell; that it insisted on views and a worship of the Deity, which to their minds was nothing else than mean, servile, and cowardly. The notion of an All-perfect, Ever-present God, in whose sight we are less than atoms, and who, while He deigns to visit us, can punish as well as bless, was abhorrent to them; they made their own minds their sanctuary, their own ideas their oracle, and conscience in morals was but parallel to genius in art, and wisdom
440 in philosophy.

6

Had I room for all that might be said upon the subject I might illustrate this intellectual religion from the history of the Emperor Julian, the apostate from Christian Truth, the foe of Christian education. He, in whom every Catholic sees the shadow of the future Anti-Christ, was all but the pattern-man of philosophical virtue. Weak points in his character he had, it is true, even in a merely poetical standard; but, take him all in all, and I cannot but recognize in him a specious beauty and nobleness of moral deportment, which combines in it the rude
450 greatness of Fabricius or Regulus with the accomplishments of Pliny or Antoninus. His simplicity of manners, his frugality, his austerity of life, his singular disdain of sensual pleasure, his military heroism, his application to business, his literary diligence, his modesty, his clemency, his accomplishments, as I view them, go to make him one of the most eminent specimens of pagan virtue which the world has ever seen. Yet how shallow, how meagre, nay, how unamiable is that virtue after all, when brought upon its critical trial by his sudden summons into the presence of his Judge! His last hours form a

unique passage in history, both as illustrating the helplessness 46ɟ
of philosophy under the stern realities of our being, and as
being reported to us on the evidence of an eye-witness.
"Friends and fellow-soldiers," he said, to use the words of a
writer, well fitted, both from his literary tastes and from his
hatred of Christianity, to be his panegyrist, "the seasonable
period of my departure is now arrived, and I discharge, with
the cheerfulness of a ready debtor, the demands of nature. . . .
I die without remorse, as I have lived without guilt. I am
pleased to reflect on the innocence of my private life; and I can
affirm with confidence that the supreme authority, that emana- 470
tion of the divine Power, has been preserved in my hands pure
and immaculate. . . . I now offer my tribute of gratitude to the
Eternal Being, who has not suffered me to perish by the
cruelty of a tyrant, but the secret dagger of conspiracy, or by
the slow tortures of lingering disease. He has given me, in the
midst of an honourable career, a splendid and glorious departure from this world, and I hold it equally absurd, equally
base, to solicit, or to decline, the stroke of fate. . . .

"He reproved the immoderate grief of the spectators, and
conjured them not to disgrace, by unmanly tears, the fate of a 480
prince who in a few moments would be united with Heaven
and with the stars. The spectators were silent; and Julian
entered into a metaphysical argument with the philosophers
Priscus and Maximus on the nature of the soul. The efforts
which he made of mind as well as body, most probably
hastened his death. His wound began to bleed with great
violence; his respiration was embarrassed by the swelling of
the veins; he called for a draught of cold water, and as soon
as he had drank it expired without pain, about the hour of
midnight." [3] Such, Gentlemen, is the final exhibition of the 490
Religion of Reason: in the insensibility of conscience, in the
ignorance of the very idea of sin, in the contemplation of his

3. Gibbon, *History of the Decline and Fall of the Roman Empire*,
Ch. 24.

own moral consistency, in the simple absence of fear, in the cloudless self-confidence, in the serene self-possession, in the cold self-satisfaction, we recognize the mere Philosopher.

7

Gibbon paints with pleasure what, conformably with the sentiments of a godless intellectualism, was an historical fulfilment of his own idea of moral perfection; Lord Shaftesbury had already drawn out that idea in a theoretical form, in his celebrated collection of Treatises which he has called "Characteristics of men, manners, opinions, views;" and it will be a further illustration of the subject before us, if you will allow me, Gentlemen, to make some extracts from his work.

One of his first attacks is directed against the doctrine of reward and punishment, as if it introduced a notion into religion inconsistent with the true apprehension of the beauty of virtue, and with the liberality and nobleness of spirit in which it should be pursued. "Men have not been content," he says, "to show the natural advantages of honesty and virtue. They have rather lessened these, the better, as they thought, to advance another foundation. They have made virtue so mercenary a thing, and have talked so much of its rewards, that one can hardly tell what there is in it, after all, which can be worth rewarding. For to be *bribed* only or *terrified* into an honest practice, bespeaks little of real honesty or worth." "If," he says elsewhere, insinuating what he dare not speak out, "if through hope merely of reward, or fear of punishment, the creature be inclined to do the good he hates, or restrained from doing the ill to which he is not otherwise in the least degree averse, there is in this case no virtue or goodness whatever. There is no more of rectitude, piety, or sanctity, in a creature thus reformed, than there is meekness or gentleness in a tiger strongly chained, or innocence and sobriety in a monkey under the discipline of the whip.... While the will is neither gained, nor the inclination wrought upon, but awe alone prevails and forces obedience, the obedience is servile, and all which is done through it merely servile." That is, he says that Christianity is the enemy of moral virtue, as influencing the mind by fear of God, not by love of good.

The motives then of hope and fear being, to say the least, 530 put far into the background, and nothing being morally good but what springs simply or mainly from a love of virtue for its own sake, this love-inspiring quality in virtue is its beauty, while a bad conscience is not much more than the sort of feeling which makes us shrink from an instrument out of tune. "Some by mere nature," he says, "others by art and practice, are masters of an ear in music, an eye in painting, a fancy in the ordinary things of ornament and grace, a judgment in proportions of all kinds, and a general good taste in most of those subjects which make the amusement and delight of the 540 ingenious people of the world. Let such gentlemen as these be as extravagant as they please, or as irregular in their morals, they must at the same time discover their *inconsistency*, live at *variance* with themselves, and in *contradiction* to that principle on which they ground their highest pleasure and entertainment. Of all other *beauties* which virtuosos pursue, poets celebrate, musicians sing, and architects or artists of whatever kind describe or form, the most delightful, the most engaging and pathetic, is that which is drawn from real life and from the passions. Nothing affects the heart like that which is 550 purely from its self, and of its own nature: such as the beauty of sentiments, the grace of actions, the turn of characters, and the *proportions and features* of a human mind. This lesson of philosophy, even a romance, a poem, or a play may teach us. . . . Let poets or the men of harmony deny, if they can, this force of nature, or withstand this *moral magic*. . . . Every one is a virtuoso of a higher or lower degree; every one pursues a grace . . . of one kind or other. The *venustum*,[4] the *honestum*,[5] the *decorum* [6] of things will force its way. . . . The most natu-

4. grace.   5. worth.   6. propriety.

560 ral beauty in the world is honesty and moral truth; for all
beauty is truth."

Accordingly, virtue being only one kind of beauty, the principle which determines what is virtuous is, not conscience, but
taste. "Could we once convince ourselves," he says, "of what
is in itself so evident, *viz.*, that in the very nature of things
there must of necessity be the foundation of a right and wrong
taste, as well in respect of inward character of features as of
outward person, behaviour, and action, we should be far more
ashamed of ignorance and wrong judgment in the former
570 than in the latter of these subjects. . . . One who aspires to the
character of a man of breeding and politeness is careful to
form his judgment of arts and sciences upon right models of
perfection. . . . He takes particular care to turn his eye from
every thing which is gaudy, luscious, and of false taste. Nor is
he less careful to turn his ear from every sort of music, besides
that which is of the best manner and truest harmony. 'Twere
to be wished we had the same regard to a *right taste in life and
manners*. . . . If civility and humanity be a taste; if brutality,
insolence, riot, be in the same manner a taste, . . . who would
580 not endeavour to force nature as well in this respect as in what
relates to a taste or judgment in other arts and sciences?"

Sometimes he distinctly contrasts this taste with principle
and conscience, and gives it the preference over them. "After
all," he says, "'*tis not merely what we call principle,* but *a
taste,* which governs men. They may think for certain, 'This
is right,' or 'that wrong;' they may believe 'this is a virtue,' or
'that a sin;' 'this is punishable by man,' or 'that by God;' yet if
the savour of things lies cross to honesty, if the fancy be florid,
and the appetite high towards the subaltern beauties and lower
590 orders of worldly symmetries and proportions, the conduct
will infallibly turn this latter way." Thus, somewhat like a
Jansenist, he makes the superior pleasure infallibly conquer,
and implies that, neglecting principle, we have but to train
the taste to a kind of beauty higher than sensual. He adds:
"*Even conscionce,* I fear, such as is owing to religious dis-

cipline, will make but a slight figure, when this taste is set amiss."

And hence the well-known doctrine of this author, that ridicule is the test of truth; for truth and virtue being beauty, and falsehood and vice deformity, and the feeling inspired by 600 deformity being that of derision, as that inspired by beauty is admiration, it follows that vice is not a thing to weep about, but to laught at. "Nothing is ridiculous," he says, "but what is deformed; nor is any thing proof against raillery but what is handsome and just. And therefore 'tis the hardest thing in the world to deny fair honesty the use of this weapon, which can never bear an edge against herself, and bears against every thing contrary."

And hence again, conscience, which intimates a Lawgiver, being superseded by a moral taste or sentiment, which has no 610 sanction beyond the constitution of our nature, it follows that our great rule is to contemplate ourselves, if we would gain a standard of life and morals. Thus he has entitled one of his Treatises a "Soliloquy," with the motto, *"Nec te quæsiveris extra;"* [7] and he observes, "The chief interest of ambition, avarice, corruption, and every sly insinuating vice, is to prevent this interview and familiarity of discourse, which is consequent upon close retirement and inward recess. 'Tis the grand artifice of villainy and lewdness, *as well as of superstition and bigotry,* to put us upon terms of greater distance and formality 620 with ourselves, and evade our *proving* method of soliloquy. . . . A passionate lover, whatever solitude he may affect, can never be truly by himself. . . . 'Tis the same reason which keeps the imaginary saint or mystic from being capable of this entertainment. Instead of looking narrowly into his own nature and mind, that he may be no longer a mystery to himself, he is taken up with *the contemplation of other mysterious natures,* which he never can explain or comprehend."

7. Seek nothing beyond yourself.

8

Taking these passages as specimens of what I call the Re-
630 ligion of Philosophy, it is obvious to observe that there is no
doctrine contained in them which is not in a certain sense true;
yet, on the other hand, that almost every statement is perverted
and made false, because it is not the whole truth. They are ex-
hibitions of truth under one aspect, and therefore insufficient;
conscience is most certainly a moral sense, but it is more; vice
again, is a deformity, but it is worse. Lord Shaftesbury may
insist, if he will, that simple and solitary fear cannot effect a
moral conversion, and we are not concerned to answer him;
but he will have a difficulty in proving that any real conversion
640 follows from a doctrine which makes virtue a mere point of
good taste, and vice vulgar and ungentlemanlike.

Such a doctrine is essentially superficial, and such will be its
effects. It has no better measure of right and wrong than that
of visible beauty and tangible fitness. Conscience indeed inflicts an acute pang, but that pang, forsooth, is irrational, and
to reverence it is an illiberal superstition. But, if we will make
light of what is deepest within us, nothing is left but to pay
homage to what is more upon the surface. To *seem* becomes
to *be;* what looks fair will be good, what causes offence will
650 be evil; virtue will be what pleases, vice what pains. As well
may we measure virtue by utility as by such a rule. Nor is this
an imaginary apprehension; we all must recollect the celebrated sentiment into which a great and wise man was betrayed, in the glowing eloquence of his valediction to the spirit
of chivalry. "It is gone," cries Mr. Burke; "that sensibility of
principle, that chastity of honour, which felt a stain like a
wound; which inspired courage, while it mitigated ferocity;
which ennobled whatever it touched, and under which *vice
lost half its evil by losing all its grossness.*" [8] In the last clause
660 of this beautiful sentence we have too apt an illustration of the
ethical temperament of a civilized age. It is detection, not the

8. Edmund Burke, *Reflections on the Revolution in France.*

sin, which is the crime; private life is sacred, and inquiry into
it is intolerable; and decency is virtue. Scandals, vulgarities,
whatever shocks, whatever disgusts, are offences of the first
order. Drinking and swearing, squalid poverty, improvidence,
laziness, slovenly disorder, make up the idea of profligacy:
poets may say any thing, however wicked, with impunity;
works of genius may be read without danger or shame, whatever their principles; fashion, celebrity, the beautiful, the
heroic, will suffice to force any evil upon the community. The 670
splendours of a court, and the charms of good society, wit,
imagination, taste, and high breeding, the *prestige* of rank,
and the resources of wealth, are a screen, an instrument, and
an apology for vice and irreligion. And thus at length we find,
surprising as the change may be, that that very refinement of
Intellectualism, which began by repelling sensuality, ends by
excusing it. Under the shadow indeed of the Church, and in
its due development, Philosophy does service to the cause of
morality; but, when it is strong enough to have a will of its
own, and is lifted up with an idea of its own importance, and 680
attempts to form a theory, and to lay down a principle, and to
carry out a system of ethics, and undertakes the moral education of the man, then it does but abet evils to which at first it
seemed instinctively opposed. True Religion is slow in
growth, and, when once planted, is difficult of dislodgement;
but its intellectual counterfeit has no root in itself: it springs
up suddenly, it suddenly withers. It appeals to what is in
nature, and it falls under the dominion of the old Adam.
Then, like dethroned princes, it keeps up a state and majesty,
when it has lost the real power. Deformity is its abhorrence; 690
accordingly, since it cannot dissuade men from vice, therefore
in order to escape the sight of its deformity, it embellishes it. It
"skins and films the ulcerous place," which it cannot probe
or heal,

> Whiles rank corruption, mining all within,
> Infects unseen.[9]

9. Shakespeare, *As You Like It*, Act III, Scene 4.

And from this shallowness of philosophical Religion it comes to pass that its disciples seem able to fulfil certain precepts of Christianity more readily and exactly than Christians themselves. St. Paul, as I have said, gives us a pattern of evangelical perfection; [10] he draws the Christian character in its most graceful form, and its most beautiful hues. He discourses of that charity which is patient and meek, humble and single-minded, disinterested, contented, and persevering. He tells us to prefer each the other before himself, to give way to each other, to abstain from rude words and evil speech, to avoid self-conceit, to be calm and grave, to be cheerful and happy, to observe peace with all men, truth and justice, courtesy and gentleness, all that is modest, amiable, virtuous, and of good repute. Such is St. Paul's exemplar of the Christian in his external relations; and, I repeat, the school of the world seems to send out living copies of this typical excellence with greater success than the Church. At this day the "gentleman" is the creation, not of Christianity, but of civilization. But the reason is obvious. The world is content with setting right the surface of things; the Church aims at regenerating the very depths of the heart. She ever begins with the beginning; and, as regards the multitude of her children, is never able to get beyond the beginning, but is continually employed in laying the foundation. She is engaged with what is essential, as previous and as introductory to the ornamental and the attractive. She is curing men and keeping them clear of mortal sin; she is "treating of justice and chastity, and the judgment to come:" she is insisting on faith and hope, and devotion, and honesty, and the elements of charity; and has so much to do with precept, that she almost leaves it to inspirations from Heaven to suggest what is of counsel and perfection. She aims at what is necessary rather than at what is desirable. She is for the many as well as for the few. She is putting souls in the way of salvation, that they may then be in a condition, if they shall be

10. I Corinthians, xiii: 1-8.

called upon, to aspire to the heroic, and to attain the full proportions, as well as the rudiments, of the beautiful.

9

Such is the method, or the policy (so to call it), of the
Church; but Philosophy looks at the matter from a very different point of view: what have Philosophers to do with the
terror of judgment or the saving of the soul? Lord Shaftesbury calls the former a sort of "panic fear." Of the latter he
scoffingly complains that "the saving of souls is now the heroic
passion of exalted spirits." Of course he is at liberty, on his
principles, to pick and choose out of Christianity what he will;   740
he discards the theological, the mysterious, the spiritual; he
makes selection of the morally or esthetically beautiful. To
him it matters not at all that he begins his teaching where he
should end it; it matters not that, instead of planting the tree,
he merely crops its flowers for his banquet; he only aims at
the present life, his philosophy dies with him; if his flowers
do but last to the end of his revel, he has nothing more to
seek. When night comes, the withered leaves may be mingled
with his own ashes; he and they will have done their work, he
and they will be no more. Certainly, it costs little to make   750
men virtuous on conditions such as these; it is like teaching
them a language or an accomplishment, to write Latin or to
play on an instrument,—the profession of an artist, not the
commission of an Apostle.

This embellishment of the exterior is almost the beginning
and the end of philosophical morality. This is why it aims at
being modest rather than humble; this is how it can be proud
at the very time that it is unassuming. To humility indeed it
does not even aspire; humility is one of the most difficult of
virtues both to attain and to ascertain. It lies close upon the   760
heart itself, and its tests are exceedingly delicate and subtle.
Its counterfeits abound; however, we are little concerned with
them here, for, I repeat, it is hardly professed even by name

in the code of ethics which we are reviewing. As has been often observed, ancient civilization had not the idea, and had no word to express it: or rather, it had the idea, and considered it a defect of mind, not a virtue, so that the word which denoted it conveyed a reproach. As to the modern world, you may gather its ignorance of it by its perversion of

770   the somewhat parallel term "condescension." Humility or condescension, viewed as a virtue of conduct, may be said to consist, as in other things, so in our placing ourselves in our thoughts on a level with our inferiors; it is not only a voluntary relinquishment of the privileges of our own station, but an actual participation or assumption of the condition of those to whom we stoop. This is true humility, to feel and to behave as if we were low; not, to cherish a notion of our importance, while we affect a low position. Such was St. Paul's humility, when he called himself "the least of the saints;" [11] such the

780   humility of those many holy men who have considered themselves the greatest of sinners. It is an abdication, as far as their own thoughts are concerned, of those prerogatives or privileges to which others deem them entitled. Now it is not a little instructive to contrast with this idea, Gentlemen,—with this theological meaning of the word "condescension,"—its proper English sense; put them in juxta-position, and you will at once see the difference between the world's humility and the humility of the Gospel. As the world uses the word, "condescension" is a stooping indeed of the person, but a bending

790   forward, unattended with any the slightest effort to leave by a single inch the seat in which it is so firmly established. It is the act of a superior, who protests to himself, while he commits it, that he is superior still, and that he is doing nothing else but an act of grace towards those on whose level, in theory, he is placing himself. And this is the nearest idea which the philosopher can form of the virtue of self-abasement; to do more than this is to his mind a meanness or an hypocrisy, and

11. Epistle to the Ephesians, iii: 8.

at once excites his suspicion and disgust. What the world is, such it has ever been; we know the contempt which the educated pagans had for the martyrs and confessors of the Church; and it is shared by the anti-Catholic bodies of this day.

Such are the ethics of Philosophy, when faithfully represented; but an age like this, not pagan, but professedly Christian, cannot venture to reprobate humility in set terms, or to make a boast of pride. Accordingly, it looks out for some expedient by which it may blind itself to the real state of the case. Humility, with its grave and self-denying attributes, it cannot love; but what is more beautiful, what more winning, than modesty? what virtue, at first sight, simulates humility so well? though what in fact is more radically distinct from it? In truth, great as is its charm, modesty is not the deepest or the most religious of virtues. Rather it is the advanced guard or sentinel of the soul militant, and watches continually over its nascent intercourse with the world about it. It goes the round of the senses; it mounts up into the countenance; it protects the eye and ear; it reigns in the voice and gesture. Its province is the outward deportment, as other virtues have relation to matters theological, others to society, and others to the mind itself. And being more superficial than other virtues, it is more easily disjoined from their company; it admits of being associated with principles or qualities naturally foreign to it, and is often made the cloak of feelings or ends for which it was never given to us. So little is it the necessary index of humility, that it is even compatible with pride. The better for the purpose of Philosophy; humble it cannot be, so forthwith modesty becomes its humility.

Pride, under such training, instead of running to waste in the education of the mind, is turned to account; it gets a new name; it is called self-respect; and ceases to be the disagreeable, uncompanionable quality which it is in itself. Though it be the motive principle of the soul, it seldom comes to view; and when it shows itself, then delicacy and gentleness are its attire, and good sense and sense of honour direct its motions. It is no

longer a restless agent, without definite aim; it has a large field of exertion assigned to it, and it subserves those social interests which it would naturally trouble. It is directed into the channel of industry, frugality, honesty, and obedience; and it becomes the very staple of the religion and morality held in honour in a day like our own. It becomes the safeguard of
840 chastity, the guarantee of veracity, in high and low; it is the very household god of society, as at present constituted, inspiring neatness and decency in the servant girl, propriety of carriage and refined manners in her mistress, uprightness, manliness, and generosity in the head of the family. It diffuses a light over town and country; it covers the soil with handsome edifices and smiling gardens; it tills the field, it stocks and embellishes the shop. It is the stimulating principle of providence on the one hand, and of free expenditure on the other; of an honourable ambition, and of elegant enjoyment. It
850 breathes upon the face of the community, and the hollow sepulchre is forthwith beautiful to look upon.

Refined by civilization which has brought it into activity, this self-respect infuses into the mind an intense horror of exposure, and a keen sensitiveness of notoriety and ridicule. It becomes the enemy of extravagances of any kind; it shrinks from what are called scenes; it has no mercy on the mock-heroic, on pretence or egotism, on verbosity in language, or what is called prosiness in conversation. It detests gross adulation; not that it tends at all to the eradication of the appetite
860 to which the flatterer ministers, but it sees the absurdity of indulging it, it understands the annoyance thereby given to others, and if a tribute must be paid to the wealthy or the powerful, it demands greater subtlety and art in the preparation. Thus vanity is changed into a more dangerous self-conceit, as being checked in its natural eruption. It teaches men to suppress their feelings, and to control their tempers, and to mitigate both the severity and the tone of their judgments. As Lord Shaftesbury would desire, it prefers playful wit and satire in putting down what is objectionable, as a more refined and

good-natured, as well as a more effectual method, than the   870
expedient which is natural to uneducated minds. It is from
this impatience of the tragic and the bombastic that it is now
quietly but energetically opposing itself to the unchristian
practice of duelling, which it brands as simply out of taste,
and as the remnant of a barbarous age; and certainly it seems
likely to effect what Religion has aimed at abolishing in vain.

10

Hence it is that it is almost a definition of a gentleman to
say he is one who never inflicts pain. This description is both
refined and, as far as it goes, accurate. He is mainly occupied
in merely removing the obstacles which hinder the free and   880
unembarrassed action of those about him; and he concurs with
their movements rather than takes the initiative himself. His
benefits may be considered as parallel to what are called comforts or conveniences in arrangements of a personal nature:
like an easy chair or a good fire, which do their part in dispel-
ling cold and fatigue, though nature provides both means of
rest and animal heat without them. The true gentleman in
like manner carefully avoids whatever may cause a jar or a jolt
in the minds of those with whom he is cast;—all clashing of
opinion, or collision of feeling, all restraint, or suspicion, or   890
gloom, or resentment; his great concern being to make every
one at their ease and at home. He has his eyes on all his company; he is tender towards the bashful, gentle towards the
distant, and merciful towards the absurd; he can recollect to
whom he is speaking; he guards against unseasonable allu-
sions, or topics which may irritate; he is seldom prominent in
conversation, and never wearisome. He makes light of favours
while he does them, and seems to be receiving when he is con-
ferring. He never speaks of himself except when compelled,
never defends himself by a mere retort, he has no ears for   900
slander or gossip, is scrupulous in imputing motives to those
who interfere with him, and interprets every thing for the

best. He is never mean or little in his disputes, never takes un-
fair advantage, never mistakes personalities or sharp sayings
for arguments, or insinuates evil which he dare not say out.
From a longsighted prudence, he observes the maxim of the ancient sage, that we should ever conduct ourselves towards our
enemy as if he were one day to be our friend. He has too much
good sense to be affronted at insults, he is too well employed to
910 remember injuries, and too indolent to bear malice. He is
patient, forbearing, and resigned, on philosophical principles;
he submits to pain, because it is inevitable, to bereavement,
because it is irreparable, and to death, because it is his destiny.
If he engages in controversy of any kind, his disciplined intellect preserves him from the blundering discourtesy of better,
perhaps, but less educated minds; who, like blunt weapons,
tear and hack instead of cutting clean, who mistake the point
in argument, waste their strength on trifles, misconceive their
adversary, and leave the question more involved than they
920 find it. He may be right or wrong in his opinion, but he is too
clear-headed to be unjust; he is as simple as he is forcible, and
as brief as he is decisive. Nowhere shall we find greater can-
dour, consideration, indulgence: he throws himself into the
minds of his opponents, he accounts for their mistakes. He
knows the weakness of human reason as well as its strength,
its province and its limits. If he be an unbeliever, he will be
too profound and large-minded to ridicule religion or to act
against it; he is too wise to be a dogmatist or fanatic in his
infidelity. He respects piety and devotion; he even supports
930 institutions as venerable, beautiful, or useful, to which he does
not assent; he honours the ministers of religion, and it contents
him to decline its mysteries without assailing or denouncing
them. He is a friend of religious toleration, and that, not only
because his philosophy has taught him to look on all forms of
faith with an impartial eye, but also from the gentleness and
effeminacy of feeling, which is the attendant on civilization.
937 Not that he may not hold a religion too, in his own way,
even when he is not a Christian. In that case his religion is one

of imagination and sentiment; it is the embodiment
ideas of the sublime, majestic, and beautiful, without
there can be no large philosophy. Sometimes he acknowledge
the being of God, sometimes he invests an unknown principle
or quality with the attributes of perfection. And this deduc-
tion of his reason, or creation of his fancy, he makes the occasion of such excellent thoughts, and the starting-point of so
varied and systematic a teaching, that he even seems like a
disciple of Christianity itself. From the very accuracy and   947
steadiness of his logical powers, he is able to see what sentiments are consistent in those who hold any religious doctrine
at all, and he appears to others to feel and to hold a whole   950
circle of theological truths, which exist in his mind no otherwise than as a number of deductions.

Such are some of the lineaments of the ethical character,
which the cultivated intellect will form, apart from religious
principle. They are seen within the pale of the Church and
without it, in holy men, and in profligate; they form the *beau-
ideal* of the world; they partly assist and partly distort the development of the Catholic. They may subserve the education
of a St. Francis de Sales or a Cardinal Pole; they may be the
limits of the contemplation of a Shaftesbury or a Gibbon.   960
Basil and Julian were fellow-students at the schools of Athens;
and one became the Saint and Doctor of the Church, the other
her scoffing and relentless foe.

Appendices

I

DISCIPLINE OF MIND

I consider, then, that the position of our minds, as far as they are uncultivated, towards intellectual objects,—I mean of our minds, before they have been disciplined and formed by the action of our reason upon them,—is analogous to that of a blind man towards the objects of vision, at the moment when eyes are for the first time given to him by the skill of the operator. Then the multitude of things, which present themselves to the sight under a multiplicity of shapes and hues, pour in upon him from the external world all at once, and are at first nothing else but lines and colours, without mutual connection, dependence, or contrast, without order or principle, without drift or meaning, and like the wrong side of a piece of tapestry or carpet. By degrees, by the sense of touch, by reaching out the hands, by walking into this maze of colours, by turning round in it, by accepting the principle of perspective, by the various slow teaching of experience, the first information of the sight is corrected, and what was an unintelligible wilderness becomes a landscape or a scene, and is understood to consist of space, and of bodies variously located in space, with such consequences as thence necessarily follow. The knowledge is at length gained of things or objects, and of their relation to each other; and it is a kind of knowledge, as is plain, which is forced upon us all from infancy, as to the blind on their first seeing, by the testimony of our other senses, and by the very necessity of supporting life; so that even the brute animals have been gifted with the faculty of acquiring it.

Such is the case as regards material objects; and it is much the same as regards intellectual. I mean that there is a vast host of matters of all kinds, which address themselves, not to the eye, but to our mental sense; viz., all those matters of thought which, in the course of life and the intercourse of society, are brought before us, which we hear of in conversation, which we read of in books; matters political, social, ecclesiastical, literary, domestic; persons, and their doings or their writings; events, and works, and undertakings, and lows, and institutions. These make up a much more subtle and intricate world than that visible universe of which I was just now speaking. It is much more difficult in this world than in the material to separate things off from each other, and to find out how they stand related to each other, and to learn how to class them, and where to locate them respectively. Still, it is not less true that, as the various figures and forms in a landscape have each its own place, and stand in this or that direction towards each other, so all the various objects which address the intellect have severally a substance of their own, and have fixed relations each of them with everything else,— relations which our minds have no power of creating, but which we are obliged to ascertain before we have a right to boast that we really know any thing about them. Yet, when the mind looks out for the first time into this manifold spiritual world, it is just as much confused and dazzled and distracted as are the eyes of the blind when they first begin to see; and it is by a long process, and with much effort and anxiety, that we begin hardly and partially to apprehend its various contents and to put each in its proper place.

We grow up from boyhood; our minds open; we go into the world; we hear what men say, or read what they put in print; and thus a profusion of matters of all kinds is discharged upon us. Some sort of an idea we have of most of them, from hearing what others say; but it is a very vague idea, probably a very mistaken idea. Young people, especially, because they are young, colour the assemblage of persons and things which they encounter with the freshness and grace of their own springtide, look for all good from the reflection of their own hopefulness, and worship what they have created. Men of ambition, again, look upon the world as a theatre for fame and

glory, and make it that magnificent scene of high enterprise and august recompence which Pindar or Cicero has delineated. Poets, too, after their wont, put their ideal interpreta-
70 tion upon all things, material as well as moral, and substitute the noble for the true. Here are various obvious instances, suggestive of the discipline which is imperative, if the mind is to grasp things as they are, and to discriminate substances from shadows. For I am not concerned merely with youth, ambition, or poetry, but with our mental condition generally. It is the fault of all of us, till we have duly practised our minds, to be unreal in our sentiments and crude in our judgments, and to be carried off by fancies, instead of being at the trouble of acquiring sound knowledge.

80   In consequence, when we hear opinions put forth on any new subject, we have no principle to guide us in balancing them; we do not know what to make of them; we turn them to and fro, and over, and back again, as if to pronounce upon them, if we could, but with no means of pronouncing. It is the same when we attempt to speak upon them: we make some random venture; or we take up the opinion of some one else, which strikes our fancy; or perhaps, with the vaguest enunciation possible of any opinion at all, we are satisfied with ourselves if we are merely able to throw off some rounded
90 sentences, to make some pointed remarks on some other subject, or to introduce some figure of speech, or flowers of rhetoric, which, instead of being the vehicle, are the mere substitute of meaning. We wish to take a part in politics, and then nothing is open to us but to follow some person, or some party, and to learn the commonplaces and the watchwords which belong to it. We hear about landed interests, and mercantile interests, and trade, and higher and lower classes, and their rights, duties, and prerogatives; and we attempt to transmit what we have received; and soon our minds become loaded
100 and perplexed by the incumbrance of ideas which we have not mastered and cannot use. We have some vague idea, for instance, that constitutional government and slavery are incon-

sistent with each other; that there is a connection between private judgment and democracy, between Christianity and civilization; we attempt to find arguments in proof, and our arguments are the most plain demonstration that we simply do not understand the things themselves of which we are professedly treating.

Reflect, gentlemen, how many disputes you must have listened to, which were interminable, because neither party understood either his opponent or himself. Consider the fortunes of an argument in a debating society, and the need there so frequently is, not simply of some clear thinker to disentangle the perplexities of thought, but of capacity in the combatants to do justice to the clearest explanations which are set before them,—so much so, that the luminous arbitration only gives rise, perhaps, to more hopeless altercation. "Is a constitutional government better for a population than an absolute rule?" What a number of points have to be clearly apprehended before we are in a position to say one word on such a question! What is meant by "constitution"? by "constitutional governmen"? by "better"? by "a population"? and by "absolutism"? The ideas represented by these various words ought, I do not say, to be as perfectly defined and located in the minds of the speakers as objects of sight in a landscape, but to be sufficiently, even though incompletely, apprehended, before they have a right to speak. "How is it that democracy can admit of slavery, as in ancient Greece?" "How can Catholicism flourish in a republic?" Now, a person who knows his ignorance will say, "These questions are beyond me;" and he tries to gain a clear notion and a firm hold of them; and, if he speaks, it is as investigating, not as deciding. On the other hand, let him never have tried to throw things together, or to discriminate between them, or to denote their peculiarities, in that case he has no hesitation in undertaking any subject, and perhaps has most to say upon those questions which are most new to him. This is why so many men are one-sided, narrow-minded, prejudiced, crotchety. This is why able men have to change their minds and their line of action in middle age, and to begin life again, because they have followed their party, instead of having secured that faculty of true perception as regards intellectual objects which has accrued to them, without their knowing how, as regards the objects of sight.

But this defect will never be corrected,—on the contrary, it will be aggravated,—by those popular institutions to which I referred just now. The displays of eloquence, or the interesting matter contained in their lectures, the variety of useful or entertaining knowledge contained in their libraries, though admirable in themselves, and advantageous to the student at a later stage of his course, never can serve as a substitute for methodical and laborious teaching. A young man of sharp and active intellect, who has had no other training, has little to show for it besides a litter of ideas heaped up into his mind anyhow. He can utter a number of truths or sophisms, as the case may be, and one is as good to him as another. He is up with a number of doctrines and a number of facts, but they are all loose and straggling, for he has no principles set up in his mind round which to aggregate and locate them. He can say a word or two on half a dozen sciences, but not a dozen words on any one. He says one thing now, and another thing presently; and when he attempts to write down distinctly what he holds upon a point in dispute, or what he understands by its terms, he breaks down, and is surprised at his failure. He sees objections more clearly than truths, and can ask a thousand questions which the wisest of men cannot answer; and withal, he has a very good opinion of himself, and is well satisfied with his attainments, and he declares against others, as opposed to the spread of knowledge altogether, who do not happen to adopt his ways of furthering it, or the opinions in which he considers it to result.

This is that barren mockery of knowledge which comes of attending on great Lecturers, or of mere acquaintance with reviews, magazines, newspapers, and other literature of the

day, which, however able and valuable in itself, is not the
instrument of intellectual education. If this is all the training
a man has, the chance is that, when a few years have passed
over his head, and he has talked to the full, he wearies of talking, and of the subjects on which he talked. He gives up the
pursuit of knowledge, and forgets what he knew, whatever it
was; and, taking things at their best, his mind is in no very   180
different condition from what it was when he first began to
improve it, as he hoped, though perhaps he never thought of
more than of amusing himself. I say, "at the best," for perhaps
he will suffer from exhaustion and a distaste of the subjects
which once pleased him; or perhaps he has suffered some real
intellectual mischief; perhaps he has contracted some serious
disorder, he has admitted some taint of scepticism, which he
will never get rid of.

And here we see what is meant by the poet's maxim, "A
little learning is a dangerous thing." Not that knowledge,   190
little or much, if it be real knowledge, is dangerous; but that
many a man considers a mere hazy view of many things to be
real knowledge, whereas it does but mislead, just as a short-
sighted man sees only so far as to be led by his uncertain sight
over the precipice.

Such, then, being true cultivation of mind, . . . consider, for
instance, what a discipline in accuracy of thought it is to have
to construe a foreign language into your own; what a still
severer and more improving exercise it is to translate from
your own into a foreign language. Consider, again, what a   200
lesson in memory and discrimination it is to get up, as it is
called, any one chapter of history. Consider what a trial of
acuteness, caution, and exactness, it is to master, and still more
to prove, a number of definitions. Again, what an exercise in
logic is classification, what an exercise in logical precision it is
to understand and enunciate the proof of any of the more difficult propositions of Euclid, or to master any one of the great
arguments for Christianity so thoroughly as to bear examination upon it; or, again, to analyze sufficiently, yet in as few

210 words as possible, a speech, or to draw up a critique upon a poem. And so of any other science,—chemistry, or comparative anatomy, or natural history; it does not matter what it is, if it be really studied and mastered, as far as it is taken up. The result is a formation of mind,—that is, a habit of order and system, a habit of referring every accession of knowledge to what we already know, and of adjusting the one with the other; and, moreover, as such a habit implies, the actual acceptance and use of certain principles as centres of thought, around which our knowledge grows and is located. Where this critical faculty

220 exists, history is no longer a mere story-book, or biography a romance; orators and publications of the day are no longer infallible authorities; eloquent diction is no longer a substitute for matter, nor bold statements, or lively descriptions, a substitute for proof. This is that faculty of perception in intellectual matters, which, as I have said so often, is analogous to the capacity we all have of mastering the multitude of lines and colours which pour in upon our eyes, and of deciding what every one of them is worth.

II

LITERATURE AND SCIENCE

Here, then, in the first place, I observe, Gentlemen, that Literature, from the derivation of the word, implies writing, not speaking; this, however, arises from the circumstance of the copiousness, variety, and public circulation of the matters of which it consists. What is spoken cannot outrun the range of the speaker's voice, and perishes in the uttering. When words are in demand to express a long course of thought, when they have to be conveyed to the ends of the earth, or perpetuated for the benefit of posterity, they must be written

down, that is, reduced to the shape of literature; still, properly 10
speaking, the terms, by which we denote this characteristic gift
of man, belong to its exhibition by means of the voice, not of
handwriting. It addresses itself, in its primary idea, to the ear,
not to the eye. We call it the power of speech, we call it language, that is, the use of the tongue; and, even when we write,
we still keep in mind what was its original instrument, for we
use freely such terms in our books as "saying," "speaking,"
"telling," "talking," "calling;" we use the terms "phraseology"
and "diction;" as if we were still addressing ourselves to the
ear.   20

Now I insist on this, because it shows that speech, and therefore literature, which is its permanent record, is essentially a
personal work. It is not some production or result, attained by
the partnership of several persons, or by machinery, or by any
natural process, but in its very idea it proceeds, and must proceed, from some one given individual. Two persons cannot
be the authors of the sounds which strike our ear; and, as they
cannot be speaking one and the same speech, neither can they
be writing one and the same lecture or discourse,—which must
certainly belong to some one person or other, and is the expres- 30
sion of that one person's ideas and feelings,—ideas and feelings
personal to himself, though others may have parallel and
similar ones,—proper to himself, in the same sense as his
voice, his air, his countenance, his carriage, and his action, are
personal. In other words, Literature expresses, not objective
truth, as it is called, but subjective; not things, but thoughts.

Now this doctrine will become clearer by considering another use of words, which does relate to objective truth, or to
things; which relates to matters, not personal, not subjective
to the individual, but which, even were there no individual 40
man in the whole world to know them or to talk about them,
would exist still. Such objects become the matter of Science,
and words indeed are used to express them, but such words
are rather symblols than language, and however many we use.

and however we may perpetuate them by writing, we never could make any kind of literature out of them, or call them by that name. Such, for instance, would be Euclid's Elements; they relate to truths universal and eternal; they are not mere thoughts, but things: they exist in themselves, not by virtue of
50 our understanding them, not in dependence upon our will, but in what is called the *nature* of things, or at least on conditions external to us. The words, then, in which they are set forth are not language, speech, literature, but rather, as I have said, symbols. And as a proof of it, you will recollect that it is possible, nay usual, to set forth the propositions of Euclid in algebraical notation, which, as all would admit, has nothing to do with literature. What is true of mathematics is true also of every study, so far forth as it is scientific; it makes use of words as the mere vehicle of things, and is thereby withdrawn from
60 the province of literature. Thus metaphysics, ethics, law, political economy, chemistry, theology, cease to be literature in the same degree as they are capable of a severe scientific treatment. And hence it is that Aristotle's works on the one hand, though at first sight literature, approach in character, at least a great number of them, to mere science; for even though the things which he treats of and exhibits may not always be real and true, yet he treats them as if they were, not as if they were the thoughts of his own mind; that is, he treats them scientifically. On the other hand, Law or Natural History has
70 before now been treated by an author with so much of colouring derived from his own mind as to become a sort of literature; this is especially seen in the instance of Theology, when it takes the shape of Pulpit Eloquence. It is seen too in historical composition, which becomes a mere specimen of chronology, or a chronicle, when divested of the philosophy, the skill, or the party and personal feelings of the particular writer. Science, then, has to do with things, literature with thoughts; science is universal, literature is personal; science uses words merely as symbols, but literature uses language in

its full compass, as including phraseology, idiom, style, com- 80
position, rhythm, eloquence, and whatever other properties
are included in it.

III

STYLE

Thought and speech are inseparable from each other. Matter and expression are parts of one: style is a thinking out into
language. This is what I have been laying down, and this is
literature; not *things,* not the verbal symbols of things; not
on the other hand mere *words;* but thoughts expressed in
language. Call to mind, Gentlemen, the meaning of the Greek
word which expresses this special prerogative of man over the
feeble intelligence of the inferior animals. It is called Logos:
what does Logos mean? it stands both for *reason* and for
speech, and it is difficult to say which it means more properly. 10
It means both at once: why? because really they cannot be
divided,—because they are in a true sense one. When we can
separate light and illumination, life and motion, the convex
and the concave of a curve, then will it be possible for thought
to tread speech under foot, and to hope to do without it—then
will it be conceivable that the vigorous and fertile intellect
should renounce its own double, its instrument of expression,
and the channel of its speculations and emotions.

Critics should consider this view of the subject before they
lay down such canons of taste as the writer [1] whose pages I 20
have quoted. Such men as he is consider fine writing to be an
addition from without to the matter treated of,—a sort of
ornament superimposed, or a luxury indulged in, by those

1. Sterne, Sermon xlii.

who have time and inclination for such vanities. They speak
as if *one* man could do the thought, and *another* the style. We
read in Persian travels of the way in which young gentlemen
go to work in the East, when they would engage in correspondence with those who inspire them with hope or fear.
They cannot write one sentence themselves; so they betake
30 themselves to the professional letter-writer. They confide to
him the object they have in view. They have a point to gain
from a superior, a favour to ask, an evil to deprecate; they have
to approach a man in power, or to make court to some beautiful lady. The professional man manufactures words for them,
as they are wanted, as a stationer sells them paper, or a school-
master might cut their pens. Thought and word are, in their
conception, two things, and thus there is a division of labour.
The man of thought comes to the man of words; and the man
of words, duly instructed in the thought, dips the pen of desire
40 into the ink of devotedness, and proceeds to spread it over the
page of desolation. Then the nightingale of affection is heard
to warble to the rose of loveliness, while the breeze of anxiety
plays around the brow of expectation. This is what the East-
erns are said to consider fine writing; and it seems pretty much
the idea of the school of critics to whom I have been referring.

We have an instance in literary history of this very proceeding nearer home, in a great University, in the latter years of
the last century. I have referred to it before now in a public
lecture elsewhere;[2] but it is too much in point here to be
50 omitted. A learned Arabic scholar had to deliver a set of lectures before its doctors and professors on an historical subject
in which his reading had lain. A linguist is conversant with
science rather than with literature; but this gentleman felt that
his lectures must not be without syle. Being of the opinion
of the Orientals, with whose writings he was familiar, he determined to buy a style. He took the step of engaging a person,
at a price, to turn the matter which he had got together into

2. *Position of Catholics in England*, Lect. III.

ornamental English. Observe, he did not wish for mere grammatical English, but for an elaborate, pretentious style. An
artist was found in the person of a country curate, and the job   60
was carried out. His lectures remain to this day, in their own
place in the protracted series of annual Discourses to which
they belong, distinguished amid a number of heavyish com-
positions by the rhetorical and ambitious diction for which he
went into the market. This learned divine, indeed, and the
author I have quoted, differ from each other in the estimate
they respectively form of literary composition; but they agree
together in this,—in considering such composition a trick and
a trade; they put it on a par with the gold plate and the flowers
and the music of a banquet, which do not make the viands   70
better, but the entertainment more pleasurable; as if language
were the hired servant, the mere mistress of the reason, and
not the lawful wife in her own house.

Bibliography

NEWMAN'S WORKS:

The Idea of a University. Edited by Charles Frederick Harrold. New York: Longmans, Green and Company, 1947.

The Rise and Progress of Universities. London: Longmans, Green and Company, 1903. This book is Volume III of "Historical Sketches."

Apologia Pro Vita Sua. Edited by C. F. Harrold. New York: Longmans, Green and Company, 1947.

BIOGRAPHICAL AND CRITICAL WORKS:

Bouyer, Louis. *Newman: His Life and Spirituality.* New York: P. J. Kenedy & Sons, 1958.

Corcoran, T. Newman's *Theory of a Liberal Education.* Dublin: 1929.

Culler, A. Dwight. *Imperial Intellect.* New Haven: Yale University Press, 1955.

Elton, Oliver. *A Survey of English Literature: 1780-1880.* Vol. III. New York: The Macmillan Company, 1920. pp. 179-217.

Harrold, Charles Frederick. *John Henry Newman: An Expository Study of His Mind, Thought and Art.* New York: Longmans, Green and Company, 1945. Chap. V.

MacDougall, Hugh A. *Acton-Newman Relations: The Dilemma of Christian Liberalism.* Bronx, N. Y.: Fordham University Press, 1962.

McGrath, Fergal. *Consecration of Learning: Lectures on Newman's Idea of a University.* Bronx, N. Y.: Fordham University Press, 1963.

May, J. Lewis. *Cardinal Newman: A Study.* New York: Dial Press, 1930. Chaps. XIV and XV.

O'Faolain, Sean. *Newman's Way.* New York: Devin-Adair Co., 1952.

Reilly, J. J. *Newman as a Man of Letters.* New York: Macmillan, 1925. Chap. vii.

Ryan, A. S. "Newman's Conception of Literature," *Critical*

Studies in Arnold, Emerson, and Newman. Iowa City: University of Iowa, 1942.

————. "The Development of Newman's Political Thought," *Review of Politics,* VII (1945), 210-240.

Trevor, Meriol. *Newman: Light in Winter.* New York: Doubleday & Co.

————. *Newman, the Pillar of the Cloud.* New York: Doubleday & Co., 1962.

Shafer, Robert. *Christianity and Naturalism.* New Haven: Yale University Press, 1926. pp. 70-120.

Stockley, W. F. P. *Newman, Education, and Ireland.* London: Sands, 1933.

Walgrave, J. H. *Newman the Theologian.* New York: Sheed & Ward, 1960.

Ward, Wilfred. *The Life of John Henry Cardinal Newman: Based on His Private Journals and Correspondence.* 2 vols. London: Longmans, Green and Company, 1912. Vol. I, chaps. xi, xii, and xiii.

GENERAL AND RELATED WORKS:

Arnold, Matthew. "Literature and Science," *Discourses in America.* New York: The Macmillan Company, 1924. (See also "Sweetness and Light," *Culture and Anarchy.* Charles Scribner's Sons, 1899.)

Hutchins, Robert Maynard. *The Higher Learning in America.* New Haven: Yale University Press, 1936.

Huxley, Thomas. "A Liberal Education and Where to Find It," "Science and Culture," "On Science and Art in Relation to Education," *Science and Education.* (Selected Works, Westminster Edition, Vol. III) New York and London: D. Appleton and Company, 1893. (*Special Note:* These chapters from Huxley should be read in connection with the chapters from Arnold listed above; these chapters comprise the essential references to a famous debate on the question of general education conducted by two of Newman's eminent contemporaries.)

Livingston, Sir Richard. *On Education.* New York: The Macmillan Company, 1944.